C000097683

CARTOG REVOLUTIONARY ANARCHISM

Michael Schmidt

AK PRESS 2013: Oakland | Edinburgh | Baltimore

Cartography of Revolutionary Anarchism
By Michael Schmidt

© 2013 Michael Schmidt
This edition © 2013 AK Press (Oakland, Edinburgh, Baltimore)

Original title: *Cartographie de l'anarchisme révolutionnaire*
© Lux Éditeur, Montréal, 2012
www.luxediteur.com
© Michael Schmidt, 2012

ISBN: 978-1-84935-138-6
e-ISBN: 978-1-84935-139-3
Library of Congress Control Number: 2013930246

AK Press	AK Press UK
674-A 23rd Street	PO Box 12766
Oakland, CA 94612	Edinburgh EH8 9YE
USA	Scotland
www.akpress.org	www.akuk.com
akpress@akpress.org	ak@akedin.demon.co.uk

The above addresses would be delighted to provide you with the latest
AK Press distribution catalog, which features several thousand books,
pamphlets, zines, audio and video recordings, and gear, all published
or distributed by AK Press. Alternately, visit our websites to browse the
catalog and find out
the latest news from the world of anarchist publishing:
www.akpress.org | www.akuk.com
revolutionbythebook.akpress.org

Printed in the United States on recycled, acid-free paper.

Cover and interior by Kate Khatib | www.manifestor.org/design
Interior compass illustration by Sean Ostrowski

CONTENTS

Pour Yolanda, Ma Pôte Monstre, qui ont rayonne la lumière

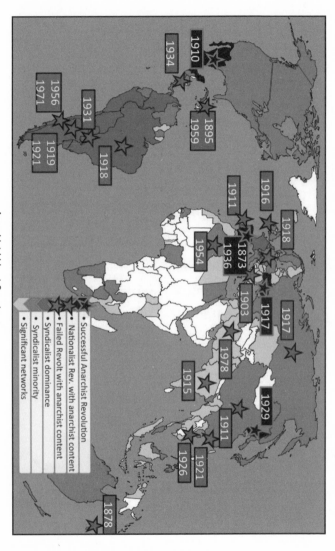

Anarchist bids at Counter-power

INTRODUCTION

The revolutionary vision of anarchism gained a foothold in the imagination of the popular classes with the rise of the anarchist strategy of revolutionary syndicalism in the trade unions affiliated to the First International.[1] It has since provided the most devastating and comprehensive critique of capitalism, landlordism, the state, and power relations in general, whether based on gender, race, or other forms of oppression. In their place it has offered a practical set of tools with which the oppressed can challenge the tiny, heavily armed elites that exploit them. Anarchism and syndicalism have been the most implacable enemies of the ruling-class industrialists and landed gentry in state and capitalist modernisation projects around the world. They have also unalterably shaped class struggle in the late nineteenth and early twentieth centuries, producing several key effects that we now presume to be fundamental aspects of civilised society.

This broad anarchist tradition had constructed, and continues to construct today, concrete projects to dissolve the centralist, hierarchical, coercive power of capital and the state, replacing it with a devolved, free-associative, horizontally federated counter-power. This concept of "counter-power" echoes that of radical feminist Nancy Fraser's "subaltern counterpublics."[2] In essence, her subaltern counterpublics are socio-political spheres separated from the mainstream, which serve as "training-grounds for agitational activities directed towards wider publics." Likewise, anarchist counter-power creates a haven for revolutionary practice that serves as a school for insurgency against the elites, a beachhead from which to launch its assault, and as the nucleus of a future, radically egalitarian society—what Buenaventura Durruti called the "new world in our hearts."[3] As Steven Hirsch notes of the Peruvian anarchist movement, they "transmitted a counter-hegemonic culture to organised labour. Through newspapers, cultural associations, sports clubs, and resistance societies they inculcated workers in anti-capitalist, anti-clerical, and anti-paternalistic beliefs. They also infused organised labour wit an ethos that stressed self-emancipation and autonomy from non-workers' groups and political parties."[4] In a sense, anarchist counter-culture provides the oppressed classes with an alternate, horizontal socio-political reality.

Beyond the factory gates, the broad anarchist tradition was among the first to systematically confront racism and ethnic discrimination. It developed an anti-racist ethic that extended from the early multi-ethnic labour struggles of the Industrial Workers of the World, through anti-fascist guerrilla movements of Europe, Asia, and Latin America in the 1920s–1950s, to become a key inspiration for the New Left in the period of African decolonisation, and later of indigenous struggles today in regions like Oaxaca in Mexico. But anarchism was more than a mere hammer to be used against prejudice: over the last one hundred and fifty years, generations of proletarians developed a complex toolkit of ideas and practices that challenged all forms of domination and exploitation. The world has changed dramatically over those decades, shaped in part by the contribution of anarcho-syndicalists and revolutionary syndicalists, a contribution usually relegated to the shadows, derided, or denied, but woven into the social fabric of contemporary society.

THE COHERENCE OF THE BROAD ANARCHIST TRADITION

Anarchism did *not* rise as a primordial rebel state of mind as far back as Lao Tzu in ancient China or Zeno in ancient Greece as many have speculated, nor was it the child of declining artisanal classes facing extinction by modern modes of production as so many Marxist writers would have us believe.[5] On the contrary, it grew within the seedbed of organised trade unions as a modern, internationalist, revolutionary socialist, and militant current with a vision of socialism-from-below, in opposition to classical Marxism's imposition of socialism-from-above.

Marxism has historically included some minority libertarian currents, such as the "Council Communists," "Left Communists," and "Sovietists" of the 1920s. However, the vast majority of historical Marxist movements strived for revolutionary dictatorship based

upon nationalisation and central planning. Every Marxist regime has been a dictatorship. Every major Marxist
party has renounced Marxism for social democracy, act-
ed as an apologist for a dictatorship, or headed a brutal
dictatorship itself. Even those mainstream Marxists who
critique the horrors of Stalin or Mao defend Lenin and
Trotsky's regime, which included all the core features of
later Marxist regimes—labour camps, a one-party dictatorship, a secret political police, terror against the peasantry, the repression of strikes, independent unions and
other leftists, etc. Marxism must be judged by history
and the authoritarian Marxist lineage that exists there-
in: not Marxism as it *might* have been, but Marxism as
it *has* been. Accordingly, I do not refer to "Stalinism"
but rather simply to Marxism or to Bolshevism in the
post–1917 period.

Over the past 15 decades, the global anarchist movement and its progeny, the syndicalist movement, have
been comprised mainly of the industrial working class—
seamen and stevedores, meat-packers and metalworkers,
construction and farm workers, sharecroppers and railwaymen—as well as of craftspeople such as shoemakers
and printers, and of peasants and indentured labourers,
with only a sprinkling of the middle classes, of doctors,
scientists, déclassé intellectuals, and journalists. It developed a sophisticated theory of how the militant minority related to broader trade unions, and to the popular
classes as a whole, seeking to move beyond an insur-
rectionary general strike (or "lock-out of the capitalist
class") to a revolutionary transformation of society. The
movement sought to achieve this through organised,
internally-democratic, worker-controlled structures, including unions, rank-and-file networks, popular militia,

street committees, consumers' co-operatives, and popular policy-making assemblies.

Many would ask what the relevance of the broad anarchist tradition would be in today's world, a world of nanotechnology and space tourism far removed from the gas-lit origins of the movement. The world has changed. In 1860, Washington D.C. was a rough, provincial town. Today, it is the unchallenged imperial capital of the world, the heart of the US "hyperpower." The telegraph had already begun to unite people, just as barbed wire divided their land—yet successful trans-Atlantic telephone cables and the Fordist production line had yet to see daylight. Many countries, notably Germany, Italy, Czechoslovakia, Poland, the Baltic and Balkan states, Vietnam, and South Africa, did not yet exist, nor did much of the Middle East. Those countries that did, like Argentina, Egypt, Algeria, and Canada, were narrow riverine or coastal strips of the giant territories they would later lay claim to. In 1860, women, even in countries as advanced as France, would have to wait a lifetime merely to secure the bourgeois vote. Serfdom and slavery were widespread, and the divine right of kings reigned supreme over vast territories, including Imperial Japan, China, and Russia, and the Ottoman and Austro-Hungarian Empires.

And yet, there are strong echoes of that world that still resonate today, for it was a world experiencing a disruptive upsurge of globalisation, evident in the colonial scramble, the ascendancy of the modern banking system, and the integration of modern industrialising economies. As the means of production modernised, shadows of unilateral military interventions in the Middle East and Central Asia were cast, and corporations wielded more power than governments in the developing world. Established societal norms broke down and the rise of terrorism, populism, religious millenarianism, and revolutionary politics took their place, as means for the oppressed to explain their pain and fight back. These phenomena are all remarkably familiar in today's world.

The broad anarchist movement has currency primarily because it remains a proletarian practise that grapples with the question of power, in relation to both intimate, interpersonal relations and the broader balance of forces in society. The anarchist conception of power is in opposition to the Marxist conception of the seizure and adaptation of coercive, vertical, centralised, bourgeois power. Instead, anarchists argue for, and in their innumerable revolts and their four main revolutions have practiced, a free, horizontal, federalist, proletarian counter-power that would equitably distribute decision-making powers and responsibilities across liberated communities. In particular, anarchist theorists have grappled with how to construct a real, living libertarian communist praxis, thereby encountering the key question facing all revolutionaries: how does the militant minority transmit the ideas of a free society to the oppressed classes, in such a way that the oppressed makes those ideas their own, moving beyond the origins of those ideas into the realm of libertarian autogestion. Central to this essay are the decisive moments in its history when the anarchist movement engaged with that very question.

In parallel to this drive to build counter-power, the early anarchist movement of the 1860s–1890s was remarkable for its deliberate construction of educational institutions everywhere that it put down roots, including rational, modernist schools in many parts of the world, and popular universities in Egypt, Cuba, Peru, Argentina, and China. The movement realised the necessity of buttressing these attempts at building structures of counter-power with a proletarian counter-culture, at creating social conditions for counter-power to flourish—by cutting the mental bonds binding the oppressed to the oppressor. While the movement aimed to cause a cultural and mental rupture between the oppressed classes and parasitic elites, they united elements of society divided by those elites: anarchist educators trained freed black slaves alongside white workers, and educated women and girls alongside men and boys, on the grounds that the oppressed of all races and genders had more in common with each other than with their exploiters.

Between 1870 and the early 1880s, the anarchist movement spread dramatically around the world, establishing anarcho-syndicalist and revolutionary syndicalist unions in Egypt, Cuba, Mexico, the US, Uruguay, Spain, and arguably in Russia. This was due in part to the fact that, until Lenin, there was no serious engagement in classical Marxism with the peasantry or the colonial world. The founders of the doctrine, Karl Marx and Friedrich Engels, had dismissed in their *Communist Manifesto* (1848) the colonised and post-colonial world as the "barbarian and semi-barbarian countries." Instead, Marxism stressed the virtues of capitalism (and even imperialism) as an onerous, yet necessary stepping stone to socialism. Engels summed up their devastating position in an article entitled "Democratic Pan-Slavism" in their *Neue Rheinische Zeitung* of 14 February 1849: the United States' annexation of Texas in 1845 and invasion of Mexico in 1846, in which Mexico lost 40% of its territory, were applauded as they had been "waged wholly and solely in the interest of civilisation," as "splendid California has been taken away from the lazy Mexicans, who could not do anything with it" by "the energetic Yankees" who would "for the first time really open the Pacific Ocean to civilisation…" Engels extended his racist polemic of inherent ethno-national virility giving rise to laudable capitalist overmastery, to argue that the failure of the Slavic nations during the 1848 Pan-European Revolt to throw off their Ottoman, Austro-Hungarian, and Russian yokes, demonstrated not only their ethnic unfitness for independence, but that they were in fact "counter-revolutionary" nations deserving of "the most determined use of terror" to suppress them.

It reads chillingly like a foreshadowing of the Nazis' racial nationalist arguments for the use of terror against the Slavs during their East European conquest. Engels' abysmal article had been written in response to *Appeal to the Slavs by a Russian Patriot* written by Mikhail Bakunin (1814–1876), a minor Russian noble who moved from a position of Pan-Slavic liberation to become, over a lifetime of militancy and clandestinity, in exile and on the barricades, anarchism's giant founding figure and Marx's most formidable opponent in defining the path to true communism; it was the dispute between their supporters that would sunder the First International in 1872 into an anarchist majority and a Marxist rump. In his *Appeal to the Slavs*, Bakunin—at that stage not yet an anarchist—had in stark contrast argued that the revolutionary and counter-revolutionary camps were divided *not* by nationality or stage of capitalist development, but by class. In 1848, revolutionary class consciousness had expressed itself as a "cry of sympathy and love for all the oppressed nationalities."[6] Urging the Slavic popular classes to "extend your had to the German people, but not to the... petit bourgeois Germans who rejoice at each misfortune that befalls the Slavs," Bakunin concluded that there were "two grand questions spontaneously posed in the first days of the [1848] spring... the social emancipation of the masses and the liberation of the oppressed nations." By 1873, when Bakunin, now unashamedly anarchist, threw down the gauntlet to imperialism, writing that "Two-thirds of humanity, 800 million Asiatics, asleep in their servitude, will necessarily awaken and begin to move," the newly-minted anarchist movement was engaging directly and repeatedly with the challenges of imperialism, colonialism, national liberation movements, and post-colonial regimes.[7]

The record of the broad anarchist movement in the pre-World War II era is dramatically more substantial than that of their Marxist contemporaries, especially in the colonial and post-colonial world.[8] The anarchist movement focused on encouraging the oppressed to start resisting immediately, without promising an imminent revolution. There was an understanding that revolutions are processes, not events, requiring a massive confluence of historical circumstances, in addition to the clear-sighted agency of the oppressed. It is because of this very early and radical challenge to colonialism and imperialism, and to the constructs of gender and race, that the anarchist movement penetrated parts of the world that Marxism did not reach until the 1920s.

THE ECONOMIC FOUNDATIONS OF ANARCHIST COUNTER-POWER

An examination of the movement's industrial and social foundations helps to explain the spread of anarchism and its appeal to the popular classes. Aside from Guiseppe

Fanelli's dramatic conversion of the bulk of the organised Spanish working class to anarchism in 1868,[9] there is probably no better example of an industrial vector of anarchism and anarcho- and revolutionary syndicalism than the Marine Transport Workers' Industrial Union (MTWIU), a section of the Industrial Workers of the World (IWW), the most international of all the syndicalist unions. The IWW had been founded in the United States in 1905, as the joint heir of the anti-racist, anti-sexist, internationalist traditions of the Knights of Labor founded in 1869, which had dominated organised American labour with a peak of 700,000 members by 1886 (weirdly, while the Knights had a large black membership, it violently opposed Chinese immigration, it also established sections in Canada and Australia, only closing up shop as a shadow of its former self in 1949), and of the explicitly anarcho-syndicalist traditions of the Central Labor Union (CLU) of 1883–1909. Despite intense repression and splits over the question of the majority's opposition to electoral politics, the IWW rose to about 250,000 members in 1917 in the US alone, and in its incarnation as the "One Big Union," perhaps 70,000 members in Canada in 1919. It was above all a movement of the poorest and most marginal workers—poor whites, immigrants, blacks, Asians, and women—many of whom worked in insecure and dangerous jobs as dockworkers, field hands, lumberjacks, miners, and factory operatives—and earned its stripes organising across racial lines in the American South. It was also an international phenomenon, with IWW groups and unions, and IWW-inspired organisations forming in Argentina, Australia, Britain, Canada, Chile, Cuba, Ecuador, Germany, Japan, New Zealand, Mexico, Peru, Siberia,

South Africa, Ukraine, and Uruguay; it had direct influence on the global labour movement as far afield as Burma, China, and Fiji; and in more recent times, it established sections in Iceland, Sweden, and Sierra Leone. In his essay on the IWW's MTWIU,[10] Hartmut Rübner writes, "Based on statistical information on the period between 1910 and 1945, the evaluated material indicates an over-proportional number of industrial actions in the sector of shipping. In many of these labour disputes, seamen exhibited a close affinity to those forms of action which are generally characterized as typically syndicalist patterns of conflict behaviour."

Asking why syndicalism was so prevalent, and why a relatively small group of revolutionary syndicalist militants could exercise such great influence, Rübner concludes that the sheer cosmopolitanism of maritime labour's

> common experiences in remote parts of the world[11] certainly created a "sense of internationalism," that helped to overcome the separations between union activists and the rank and file… In the harbour districts, the seafaring-reliant community maintained a tight-knit communication network that provided the individual seaman with the necessary information interchange to accomplish recreation and job opportunities. Loadinghouses, employment agencies, hiring halls, trade union offices and International Seamen's Clubs were situated in the direct neighbourhood of the docklands. When conflict situations arose, the localities and meeting places of the harbour districts often functioned as initial positions for collective strike activities.

This docklands community was not automatically progressive or revolutionary, but as Rübner notes, traditional socialist and union organisers tended to shy away from organising there, leaving the field open to proletarian revolutionary syndicalists. Moreover, the strongly anti-racist stance of the revolutionary syndicalists stood in sharp contrast to those of the traditional unions, in keeping with the seafaring and longshoring communities, where discrimination made no sense. In fact, he argues that the strength of "syndicalism in shipping should be seen in correlation to the dwindling attractiveness of exclusive trade union policies" that weakened workers' power by splintering them into ethnic groupings. On the other hand, according to Rübner,

> syndicalism promoted a programmatic internationalism and placed its perspectives upon the idea of a multinational counterpole to the interconnections of capital... [and] Organizations like the Industrial Workers of the World (IWW) offered access for the semiqualified or non-white workforce. Due to this accessibility, the IWW scored their first organizational successes amongst those black and Hispanic seamen and dockworkers, formerly neglected by the exclusive and chauvinist union policy. An indication for the outgrowth of seamen's radicalism can be seen in the fact, that maritime [revolutionary] syndicalism had gained remarkable strongholds in France, Netherlands, Italy and the USA before 1914. Through seafaring members of the IWW ("Wobblies") and returning immigrants, the idea of industrial unionism spread over to Australasia, Latin America and Europe. In the aftermath of the war,

the Maritime Transport Workers' Industrial Union
No.510 of the IWW developed to be the driving
force behind international maritime syndicalism…
Between 1919 and 1921, maritime syndicalism
overrode its minority position and became a factor
to be seriously reckoned with."

Thus, maritime revolutionary syndicalism both
counteracted the economic concentration of the industry and rose to meet the challenge of the motor-
isation of shipping. While Rübner incorrectly writes
of the MTWIU's "centralized industrial unionism,"
rather than its decentralised structure, he recognises its
superiority over the outmoded craft unionism of competing mainstream unions, and notes that the union's
"elementary council democracy" was based on "'ship's
committees.' Its delegates were supposed to cooper-
ate with the dockworkers in a common 'port district
council.' This model of 'industrial communism' which
[was] based on regional councils connected to an 'international headquarters,' was implemented to overcome the 'national frontiers.'"

In Rübner's final analysis of why maritime revolutionary syndicalism lost the high ground of the early
1920s, he says that, firstly, the revolutionary syndicalists were excluded from new corporatist arrangements
implemented in many countries, and, secondly, despite
their flexible approach to modernisation, crew reduc-
tions and the redundancy of entire classes of maritime
labour (such as the firemen and coal trimmers) put
members out of work. Lastly, the general dilution of
radicalism ashore seriously undercut the ability of the
anarcho- and revolutionary syndicalist cause to stay

afloat. Rübner does recognise that "syndicalism displayed its greatest effects in its attempt to overcome both the divisions in craft as well as... ethnic segregation... [but] failed to stabilise radical workplace militancy in a lasting framework."

Rübner goes on to admit that the Marxist movement stepped into the vacuum, but could only do so by "implementing the proven parts of the syndicalist strategy," including ship's committees. Today, as the corporatist labour arrangements that sustained the status quo in both Marxist and right-wing dictatorships collapse, and neoliberal austerity bites deep into the welfare gains once assured elsewhere, many workers are again as industrially excluded as their forebears were. And thus, revolutionary syndicalism, sometimes under the mentorship of the old anarcho- and revolutionary syndicalist unions and traditions, is being rediscovered as a means of shifting power back onto the shopfloor. As globalisation creates conditions whereby, for example, Bangladeshis are working for slave wages in Sudan, the appeal of anarcho- and revolutionary syndicalism's multi-ethnic approach is becoming viable again.

THE SOCIAL FOUNDATIONS OF ANARCHIST COUNTER-POWER

The social conditions in which workers live, and not only their working life, contribute greatly to their understanding of the world, and inform the methods they adopt to defend their interests. Bert Altena offers insight into the importance of class and culture in various communities of workers, in determining whether anarchism and anarcho- and revolutionary syndicalism gained a foothold within them.[12]

As Altena states,

revolutionary syndicalism contains [both] an authentic labour movement and one with a tradition. Revolutionary syndicalism was in fact either a continuation of very old labour movements or, as I will argue, a phenomenon in which the world of the workers was isolated from the rest of society. In these circumstances, workers generally had to rely on themselves for social security and they could develop their own workers' culture. Parliamentary politics belonged to the world of the bourgeoisie, which was completely foreign to workers... The anarchists, who during the 1880s and 1890s saw that their strategy of insurrection and terror did not help their cause, brought to these workers only a sharper theoretical articulation of their beliefs by introducing them to the concepts of the general strike, direct action, the value of action by workers themselves, the importance of direct democracy. They also gave them a broader cultural perspective. They only taught the workers to state more clearly what they already thought, to do better what they already practiced and they brought them the perspective of a class society beyond the local sphere.

Altena takes as his examples two neighbouring towns of equal size (approximately 20,000 residents) in the Netherlands in 1899: the industrial port town of Flushing; and the local government seat and market town of Middelburg, a mere six kilometres away. At this time, Dutch anarcho-syndicalism was enjoying its first successes, evidenced by the growth of the National Workers' Secretariat (NAS), and Flushing was dominated by one big shipyard, while other employment was to be found on the docks or on the ferry to England. By comparison, Middelburg had small construction yards, a metalworks, and a timber company. According to Altena,

> As a result of the town's economy, the social structure of Flushing consisted of a broad working-class base, a rather small layer of middle classes (shopkeepers, teachers and clerical workers) and a very small elite. The social structure of Middelburg was much less lopsided and at the same time more differentiated. The town had a rather broad layer of shopkeepers. The educated middle classes were much stronger because of Middelburg's function as the administrative and judicial centre of the province and its rich collection of educational institutions. The elite of Middelburg (gentry, magistrates and some entrepreneurs) consequently was much larger and more strongly represented in the town than its equivalent in Flushing.

The shopkeepers in Flushing were pretty poor themselves, so the class function they could have performed as social middlemen between workers and the elite was weak. The municipality itself was too impoverished to assist workers in times of crisis, forcing them to rely on themselves. By comparison, in Middelburg, the broad middle class produced many social-democrat teachers, artisanal entrepreneurs, and lawyers, who not only provided the workers with a social connection to the elite, but who, enabled by the town's greater wealth, could assist the workers in troubled times. As Altena notes,

> Socialism appeared in Flushing much earlier (1879) than it did in Middelburg and it was entirely a

working class affair. It developed in a libertarian direction. For the next forty years the labour movement of Flushing would be dominated by revolutionary syndicalism. It proved extremely difficult to establish a branch of the social-democratic party in this working-class town. Only in 1906 a tiny and weak branch was set up. The revolutionary syndicalists, however, developed a rich culture: choirs, a freethought union with its own library, musical societies and a very good theatrical club, which performed an ambitious repertoire... it was much easier to keep the syndicalist principle intact with the help of cultural activities than on the shopfloor only... Flushing presented no problem to the syndicalists in further developing their cultural activities. Bourgeois cultural life, with its own concerts, plays and libraries hardly existed in the town.

By comparison, in Middelburg, "After 1895, even their [the workers'] own branch of the social-democratic party was dominated by socialists from bourgeois origins... The workers of Middelburg not only found it much more difficult to develop an independent culture of their own, independence was also repressed on the shopfloor." In Middelburg, where women often worked as maids in the houses of the wealthy, a working-class attitude of servility was cultivated, whereas in Flushing, where women were active and visible anarchists/syndicalists, workers' pride in their skills, established through job control, was high. Altena concludes that working-class *cultural* counter-power is as important to the attractiveness of anarchism and anarcho- and revolutionary syndicalism (which he equates) as its *industrial* counter-power. "When workers can build a world of their own, the choice for syndicalism is a logical, though not a necessary one. This could explain why syndicalist movements tend to appear in mono-industrial, company towns…," according to Altena.

This was certainly true of, say, the mining towns of the American Midwest, where the IWW became a force to be reckoned with, but not in the more economically diversified worlds of port cities, where anarcho- and revolutionary syndicalism entrenched itself, except to the extent that maritime workers formed their own subculture, distinct from their neighbouring railwaymen and meat-packers—as within the maritime workers, the cooks and the stokers performed different social as well as industrial roles. Altena argues that, whereas syndicalism created an alternate world for workers, the mainstream social-democratic and Christian unions, especially through parliamentarism, "integrated workers into the political structures and processes of the country." Except in countries where they were forced to act much like the syndicalists, as an illegal counter-power, the Marxist unions also served to integrate workers into the needs of capital and the state, instead of standing opposed to it.

As Altena notes,

> In cultural activities too the syndicalists were confronted with competitors: sports (which many syndicalists disliked because sports diverted from the essential struggle of the workers) or 'capitalist' forms of entertainment such as movies and dancing. The radio challenged the syndicalist music and theatre with "real" professional culture and made them look poor and amateurish. Possibly the most important

factor was that syndicalist culture was intimately intertwined with the movement as a whole. It was always imbued with syndicalist norms and it pointed to the big syndicalist goal. As soon as syndicalism lost the realisability of its vision, its culture became hollow because its message became hollow... In so far as the syndicalists did not abandon their principles or disbanded, they had to accept marginalization. Marginal movements, however, can still be very useful movements.

ASSESSING ANARCHIST/SYNDICALIST HISTORY IN FIVE WAVES

From a long-term perspective, the fortunes of the broad anarchist tradition—like those of the militant, autonomous working class itself—rise and fall in waves. The nature of these waves is a complex textile, entwining the weft of working class culture and activity with the warp of capital in crisis, and the ebb and flow of the global movements of people, capital and ideas.

However, anarchist historiography has been distorted by the myth of the "Five Highlights" or the crude potted history by which many anarchists understand the high-water marks of their movement: the Haymarket Martyrs of 1887;[13] the French General Confederation of Labour's 1906 *Charter of Amiens*;[14] the Kronstadt Uprising of 1921;[15] the Spanish Revolution of 1936–1939;[16] and the "French" Revolt of 1968.[17] This anaemic version of anarchism's history suffers from a confused notion of what anarchism is, by, for instance, over-inflating anarchist involvement in the Kronstadt and Parisian Revolts, where anarchist influence was marginal, and accepting the verdict of hostile state socialists, by, for example, caricaturing the Ukrainian Revolution as an adventurist peasant sideshow of the Russian Revolution. It also completely ignores other Revolutions impacted by a major anarchist influence, such as Morelos and Baja California, Mexico in 1910–1920 (where anarchist praxis was influential), the Shinmin Prefecture of Manchuria in 1929–1931 (where the constructive anarchist social experiment was profound), and the Escambray Mountains and underground trade unions of Cuba in 1952–1959 (where mass anarchist traditions ran eight decades deep), as well as several urban anarchist communes, including in southern Spain in 1873–1874, in the mountains of Macedonia in 1903, and in the port city of Guangzhou in southern China in 1921–1923.

The most obvious weakness of this history, however, is that it is notably North Atlanticist, and ignores even the significant Dutch, Scandinavian, and Eastern European anarchist movements.[18] A far more important omission is the massive Latin anarchist and anarcho- and revolutionary syndicalist movements which dominated the organised working classes of Cuba, Mexico, Brazil, Portugal, Argentina, and Uruguay—which I will detail later in this essay. Also excluded are the powerful East Asian anarchist currents. Lastly, there was the key role played by anarchist militants in establishing the first trade unions and articulating the early revolutionary socialist discourse in North and Southern Africa,[19] the Caribbean and Central America,[20] Australasia,[21] South-East Asia,[22] South Asia,[23] and the Middle East.[24]

To take a few examples: the initially anarchist anticolonial Ghadar (Mutiny) Party, established in 1913, built a world-spanning movement that not only established roots on the Indian subcontinent in Hindustan and Punjab, but which linked radicals within the Indian Diaspora as far afield as Afghanistan, British East Africa (Uganda and Kenya), British Guiana (Guiana), Burma, Canada, China, Fiji, Hong Kong, Japan, Malaya (Malaysia), Mesopotamia (Iraq), Panama, the Philippines, Siam (Thailand), Singapore, South Africa, and the USA, with Ghadarites remaining active in Afghanistan into the 1930s and in colonial Kenya into the 1950s—after Indian independence; meanwhile, in South Africa, a constellation of revolutionary syndicalist organisations such as the Industrial Workers of Africa (IWA) and the Indian Workers' Industrial Union (IWIU) were explicitly built on IWW lines for people of colour in 1917–1919, and consolidated into a single organisation, the ideologically mixed Industrial and Commercial Union (ICU), which peaked at 100,000 members in 1927, but which created sections in South-West Africa (Namibia) in 1920, in Southern Rhodesia (Zimbabwe) in 1927—which survived into the 1950s—and in Northern Rhodesia (Zambia) in 1931; lastly, from 1907, a Socialist Federation of Australasia (SFA) began spreading syndicalist ideas in Australia and New Zealand, with the result that in Australia, the IWW established itself in 1910, becoming the most influential radical labour tendency, albeit a minority one, peaking at perhaps 2,000 members in 1916, surviving into the 1930s, while in New Zealand, the IWW-influenced New Zealand Federation of Labour (NZFL) was founded in 1911 and within a year, the "Red Fed" numbered all the unionised miners and dockworkers in its ranks, had 15,000 members; given the small size of the New Zealand population, the "Red Fed" was—in relative terms—fifteen times larger than the American IWW; overshadowed by

the reformist federation, New Zealand syndicalist tradition would nevertheless fight a last-ditch defence during
the great waterfront lockout of 1955.

In other words, "Five Highlights" is largely a mar-
tyrology and a museum-piece, a quasi-religious tragedy
recited like an anarchist rosary, thereby reducing the
broad anarchist tradition to an honourable, yet failed,
minority tradition of romantically doomed resistance.
This convention must be replaced with a far broader,
balanced narrative of the movement's triumphs and
tragedies, one that demonstrates its universal adaptability and its global reach, its overwhelming dominance in
the organised labour movements of many countries, its
numerous revolts against capital and the state, its break-
throughs in fighting for labour rights, gender equality,
and against racism and imperialism, its successful revolutionary experiments in building a new society in the
shell of the old, its complexities, challenges, and numerous arguments over tactics and strategies, and its mul-
ti-generational lines of ideological and organisational
descent, as well as its current relevance.

Instead of this impoverished convention—which
excludes the early anarcho- and revolutionary syndicalist trade unions of Cuba, Mexico, Spain, the United
States, and Uruguay in the 1870s and 1880s—I prefer
to speak of "Five Waves" of anarchist and anarcho- and
revolutionary syndicalist militancy that rose and fell in
accordance with a more general expansion and contraction of objective conditions for the organised popular
classes. In the first volume of *Counter-power*,[25] linkages
between the poorly-understood international First Wave
of 1868–1894 and the far better studied Second Wave
of 1895–1923, including the Revolutions in Mexico,

Russia and Ukraine, are discussed, and I will explore them in greater depth in this essay. In the forth-coming Volume 2 of *Counter-power*,[26] we will examine the equally famous Third Wave of 1924–1949, which embraces the Revolutions in Manchuria and Spain and which, together with the Second Wave, constitutes anarchism's "Glorious Period." Discussion will also focus on the Fourth Wave of 1950–1989, which peaked with the Cuban Revolution in 1952–1959 and again with the New Left of 1968, and the current Fifth Wave, generated in 1989 by the fall of the Berlin Wall, and the rising "horizontalist" challenge to hoary old Soviet-style Marxist "communism" (in reality, authoritarian state capitalism), right-wing dictatorship, and neoliberalism by the new movements of the globalised popular classes. Our "Five Waves" theory is, however, meant as a historical guide to high- and low-water marks, not as an ironclad law of cyclical progress and reaction.

Firstly, our approach in *Counter-power* expands the history of the broader anarchist movement beyond the limitations of the "Five Highlights," which presuppose an initial prominence through the French CGT of the early 1900s, and a death on the barricades of Barcelona in 1939, with a belated last gasp in 1968. Secondly, it extends the movement's geographical range beyond the usual West European and North American territories to the furthest reaches of the earth. By means of this approach, adequately supported by primary research, we debunk the common notion of "Spanish exceptionalism": the false idea that only in Spain did anarchism achieve anything like a mass movement of the popular classes. We also show the universality of the anarchist message, a message that, while it was adapted to local circumstance, and which, like all political tendencies, has its aberrations and betrayals, remained and remains largely coherent and intact across space and time, relevant to oppressed people everywhere.

DEFINING ANARCHISM, ANARCHO-SYNDICALISM, AND REVOLUTIONARY SYNDICALISM

This essay is very far from a total history of the movement. It merely sketches the broader outlines of the Five Waves theory. The anarchist texts quoted do not form a holy canon, but rather indicate how, at decisive moments, the movement grappled with the complex question at the heart of making a social revolution, which has vexed all leftist revolutionaries: what is the relationship between the specific revolutionary organisation and the mass of the exploited and oppressed. It is also deliberately imbalanced, for it is unnecessary to rehash the wealth of knowledge on, for instance, the French and Spanish anarcho- and revolutionary syndicalist movements. Rather, the emphasis is on the comparatively larger but understudied Latin American anarchist and syndicalist movements, as well as the powerful and significant, yet often unknown, movements in regions such as South-East Asia or North and Southern Africa.

First, however, we need to define what precisely we mean by "anarchism" and a vision of "libertarian communism," although these are sometimes held to be two distinct tendencies (a distinction we find too fine and unconvincing). The term "anarchist-communism," often opposed to plain "anarchism" and also opposed to anarcho- and revolutionary syndicalism, has been used quite differently, in different circumstances, in different eras. In *Black Flame*, we show that it is false to set up a dichotomy between anarcho- and revolutionary syndicalism and "anarchist-communism"—we prefer the overarching term "anarchism." As we write: "Not only is this alleged distinction absent from the bulk of anarchist writings until recently, but it also simply does not work as a description of different tendencies within the broad anarchist tradition. Moreover, the vast majority of people described in the literature as 'anarchist communists' or 'anarcho-communists' championed syndicalism... On the other hand, the majority of syndicalists endorsed 'anarchist communism' in the sense of a stateless socialist society based on the communist principle of distribution according to need. It is difficult to identify a distinct 'anarchist-communist' strategy or tendency that can be applied as a useful category of anarchism."

Instead, we develop a distinction within the broad anarchist tradition between two main *strategic* approaches, which we call "mass anarchism" and "insurrectionist anarchism." Mass anarchism stresses that only mass movements can create a revolutionary change in society and are typically built by formal, directly-democratic organisations, such as revolutionary syndicalist unions, through struggles about bread-and-butter issues and immediate reforms. Anarchists must participate in such movements, to radicalise and transform them into levers of revolutionary change. Critically, reforms are won *from below* and act as a "revolutionary gymnasium," preparing the masses for taking power in their own right. These victories must be distinguished from reforms applied from above, which undermine popular movements. The insurrectionist approach, in contrast, claims that reforms are illusory, that even revolutionary syndicalist unions are willing or unwitting bulwarks of the existing order, and that formal organisations are automatically authoritarian. Consequently, insurrectionist anarchism emphasises catalytic, armed action by small "affinity groups" (such action called "propaganda by the deed") as the most important means of provoking a spontaneous revolutionary upsurge by the masses. What distinguishes insurrectionist anarchism from mass anarchism is not necessarily violence, as such, but its place in strategy. For insurrectionist anarchism, propaganda by the deed, carried out by conscious anarchists, is seen as a means of generating a mass movement; for most mass anarchism, violence operates as a means of self-defence for an *existing* mass movement.

By syndicalism, we mean a revolutionary anarchist trade union strategy, which views unions—structured around participatory democracy and a revolutionary vision of libertarian communism—as a key means to resist the ruling class in the here-and-now, and as the nucleus of a new social order of self-management, democratic economic planning, and universal human community. The "anarcho-syndicalists" explicitly root their politics and practices within the anarchist tradition, whereas the "revolutionary syndicalists" avoid the anarchist label, either for tactical reasons, or due to ignorance about the anarchist roots of syndicalism. Both are simply variants of a basic revolutionary trade union approach. That approach, as previously argued, was developed by the anarchists of the First International. Anarcho-syndicalism and revolutionary syndicalism are both part of a key mass anarchist strategy of building revolutionary counter-power and revolutionary counter-culture. The anarchist tradition, including all of anarcho- and revolutionary syndicalism, is what we refer to as the "broad anarchist tradition."

In this essay, an "anarchist-communist" versus anarcho- or revolutionary syndicalist binary will not be used to frame the issues discussed. However, I will highlight at key points an important thread in anarchist theory and strategy: the question of whether anarchists and syndicalists need political groups dedicated to the promotion of the ideas of the broad anarchist tradition, and, if so, what form such groups should take. When the editors of the Paris-based, anarchist newspaper *Dielo Truda* (*Workers' Cause*) issued the *Organisational Platform of the Libertarian Communists* in 1926, they were met by a storm of controversy. Some anarchists saw the editors' advocacy of a unified anarchist political organisation with collective discipline as an attempt to 'Bolshevise' anarchism, and accused its primary authors, Pyotr Arshinov and Nestor Makhno, of going over to classical Marxism. Nestor Makhno (1889–1934), born a peasant in small-town south-eastern Ukraine, was imprisoned in 1908 for terrorist actions, freed during the Russian Revolution in 1917, and established the Group of Anarchist Communists (GAK) and the Union of Peasants in his home town. Widely recognised as a brilliant military strategist, the libertarian armed forces that he established, the Revolutionary Insurgent Army of the Ukraine (RPAU), successfully defeated the Central Powers, Ukrainian nationalist, and White monarchist armies, before being betrayed by the Red Army. He died in exile in Paris of tuberculosis.[27] Pyotr Arshinov, sometimes rendered Archinov (1887–1937), was a Ukrainian anarchist metalworker, who was jailed for 20 years for arms smuggling. He met Nestor Makhno in prison, and went on to become a co-founder of the Alarm Confederation of Anarchist Organisations (Nabat), and the key partisan historian of the Makhnovist movement. Having escaped into exile in Paris, he returned to Russia in 1935 where he was murdered during Stalin's purges for "attempting to restore anarchism in Russia."

But Makhno's and Arshinov's idea, essentially, originates with Bakunin, and may be called a Bakuninist dual organisationist strategy. Namely, this is the idea that a revolutionary anarchist/syndicalist movement requires *two* distinct types of organisation: revolutionary mass organisations of the oppressed classes, open to all working and poor people, including a revolutionary anarchist/syndicalist line to form the bases of counterpower; and specific, exclusive, anarchist/syndicalist political organisations, based on tight political agreement. The former are the mass movements that can overthrow the system; the latter are the specific political organisations that systematically promote revolutionary anarchist/syndicalist ideas through engagement with the popular classes, ranging from propaganda to political struggles within the mass organisations.

Thus in *Black Flame*, we argue that the *Platform* and "Platformism" were not a break with the anarchist tradition, but rather a fairly orthodox *restatement* of well-established views. From the time of Bakunin, himself part of the anarchist International Alliance of Socialist Democracy operating within the First International, the great majority of anarchists and anarcho- and revolutionary syndicalists advocated the formation of specific anarchist political groups *in addition* to mass organisations, such as syndicalist unions, peasant soviets, workers' militia, neighbourhood assemblies, and others. In other words, most supported organisational dualism: the mass organisation, such as a union, must work in tandem with specifically anarchist and syndicalist political organisations. Moreover, most believed that these groups should have fairly homogeneous, principled, strategic, and tactical positions, as well as some form of organisational discipline. Today, the term "anarchist-communism" is sometimes used to refer to the Bakuninist dual-organisationist approach. This is notable especially in Western Europe and North America, whereas in regions such as Latin America, terms such as Bakuninist and *especifismo* (specificity) are preferred. Due, however, to the confusion surrounding the term "anarchist-communism," I have chosen to avoid the term wherever possible.

The First Wave (1868–1894): Emergence

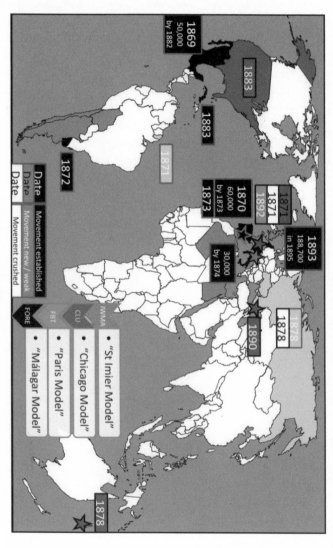

THE FIRST WAVE, 1868–1894

THE RISE OF THE BROAD ANARCHIST/SYNDICALIST
MOVEMENT IN THE ERA OF STATE
AND CAPITALIST EXPANSION

Looking briefly at the family tree of the broad anarchist movement and its watershed dates, the French Revolution of 1793 gave rise to radical republicanism, which embraced both Jacobin authoritarianism on the "right," and *Enrage* libertarianism on the "left." As a result of the Pan-European Revolt of 1848, a distinct socialist current, containing contradictory tendencies, branched out from radical republicanism, the contradictions coming to a head in 1868, with the separation of distinct anarchist majority and Marxist minority currents within the First International. Marxism would further divide into moderate Menshevik and radical Bolshevik strands in the Russian Revolt of 1905–1906. Earlier, in 1881, an anarcho-insurrectionary minority favouring armed struggle had branched off to the left of the anarchist working class majority, approximating in many respects, in its purism and immediatism, the tiny "left communist," "council communist," and "sovietist" tendencies that split to the left of Leninism in Germany, Italy, France, the Netherlands, Bulgaria, and Britain during the period between 1918 and 1923.

The mass tendency of anarchism arose during an expansive phase of modern capitalism in the 1860s, when imperialist pioneers began their surge into the unconquered half of North America, and turned their greedy eyes towards the material—and human—resources of Africa, Latin America, China, and elsewhere. It arose from the ghettos of the newly-industrialised proletariat, in the heartland of imperialism and its key raw material producing nations, and its first decades infused everyone from déclassé intellectuals to Mexican peasants with its raw self-empowerment. The founding in 1864 of the International Working Men's Association (IWMA), or First International, realised all of the pre-conditions for revolutionary anarchism/syndicalism: important sections of the working class and peasantry had achieved an internationalist, revolutionary consciousness, and created a transnational federation of their own organisations, primarily based on organised labour. The proto-anarchist, libertarian socialist mutualism of Pierre-Joseph Proudhon, son of a barrel-maker, rapidly established itself as the major current in the IWMA, but was just as swiftly supplanted by its natural matured expression: anarchism/syndicalism under the influence of Mikhail Bakunin and his circle. The main wellsprings of

anarchist-communism within the IWMA were the IW-
MA's worker organisations themselves, aided and abet-
ted by the International Brotherhood (IB) established
by Bakunin in 1864, and replaced in 1868 by his International Alliance of Socialist Democracy (IASD).[28]

So it was that a First Wave of anarcho- and revolutionary syndicalist organisations sprang up: the Spanish Regional Federation (FRE), was founded in 1870
by workers radicalised by IB agent Giuseppe Fanelli,
peaked at 60,000 members by 1873 when it ran several
cities in southern Spain during the Cantonalist Revolt,
making it the largest section of the First International,
was revived in 1881 after the post-Revolt repression as
the Spanish Regional Labour Federation (FTRE), the
largest section of the anarchist "Black International,"
but was repressed in 1889, revived in 1891 under the
influence of the Spanish Regional Anarchist Organisation (OARE) as the Pact of Union & Solidarity (PUS),
but repressed again, a cycle that would repeat until anarcho-syndicalism rooted itself intractably in 1910 with
the foundation of the famous National Confederation
of Labour (CNT).[29] The early syndicalist Proletarian
Circle (CP) in Mexico founded in 1869, became the
Grand Circle of Workers (GCO) the following year
with a significant anarchist presence, growing to 10,000
members within five years, then a parallel Grand Circle
of Mexican Workers (GCOM) was established in 1876,
with the anarchists in control of both organisations,
representing the bulk of the organised Mexican working class, by 1881 (the CGO attained 15,000 members,
while the GCOM attained 50,000 members and affiliated to the "Black International"). Both were repressed
in 1882, but the GCOM was revived as the Grand

Circle of Free Labour (GCOL) in the early 1900s, but was swiftly crushed, the syndicalist movement only reviving in 1912 during the Mexican Revolution.[30] The Regional Federation of the Eastern Republic of Uruguay (FRROU) was founded in 1872, affiliated to the anarchist wing of the First International, and was followed in 1885 by an anarcho-syndicalist Worker's Federation (FO).[31] In Cuba, the syndicalist Artisan's Central Council (JCA) was founded in 1883, becoming reorganised as the Labourer's Circle (CT) in 1885, followed by a string of initiatives culminating in the establishment of the anarcho-syndicalist Cuban Labour Confederation (CTC) in 1895.[32] And lastly, in the US, the anarcho-syndicalist Central Labor Union (CLU) in was founded in 1883 (in anticipation of what would become a key anarchist strategy in the twentieth century, the CLU was established by and worked closely with an anarchist-insurrectionist "political" organisation, the International Working Person's Association, IWPA, which was affiliated to the anarchist "Black International," and grew to about 5,000 members, surviving in much-reduced form until the First World War).[33] The short-lived Northern Workers' Union (NWU) established in Russia in 1878 was arguably part of this First Wave: echoing anarchists like Bakunin, the NWU demanded the abolition of the state and its replacement by a federation of industrial and agrarian communes, but took what could be seen later as an essentially De Leonist[34] line in proposing the parallel tactic of working-class domination of a constituent assembly.

The significance of this First Wave of anarcho- and revolutionary syndicalist organising needs to be underlined—not least by comparing the sheer size of these working class organisations to the meagre 1,000 members *world-wide* who were affiliated to the Marxist rump of the First International at the time. Firstly, it is important to note that of the five countries where this First Wave entrenched itself, three were later to experience revolutions with significant anarchist involvement. In Cuba, the anarcho-syndicalist movement dominated the working class for 50 years, until the late 1920s, with a significant revival in the late 1930s and again in the mid–1940s, until its key, but usually ignored, role in the unions during the Cuban Revolution of 1952–1959. In Mexico, the movement was involved in the armed peasant risings in 1869 and in 1878, dominated the unions in the 1910s, and was the primary engine behind the revolutionary peak of 1915–1916. In Spain, the movement had a continuous trade union presence, in the FRE of the 1860s, continuing on in five different organisational incarnations, each suppressed in turn, until the formation of the famous National Confederation of Labour (CNT) in 1910, and onwards into the 1930s, when it became the most important revolutionary player in Spain. In Uruguay, the movement dominated organised labour in the early twentieth century, and remained a strong enough minority current to re-establish the dominant union centre in the 1960s, and to engage in guerrilla warfare and underground student work against the state between 1968 and 1976. In the USA, however, revolutionary syndicalism never grew to be anything more than a militant minority tendency, overshadowed by more reformist unions. In Imperial Russia, the movement was swiftly crushed, and it would take more than a generation to establish a minority anarchist presence in the trade unions there.[35]

Secondly, the presence of non-European organisations in this First Wave undermines the convention that anarcho-syndicalism—the application of anarchist federalism and direct democracy to the trade union movement—was a "French invention" of the 1890s, and emphasises its adaptability and applicability to countries as industrialised and sovereign as the USA or as agrarian and colonised as Cuba. In other words, it arose in both the global North and the global South, in concentrations of expansive industrial and commercial agricultural growth—but not among the declining artisanal classes, as Marxists often claim. Its social vectors were those of the intense upheaval created by a massive, constant movement of workers around the world to satisfy new growth, and the loss of political control experienced by the old landed oligarchies, the *latifundistas*, resulting from the rise of a modernising bourgeoisie and state bureaucracy, the inevitable corollary of which was the rise of a militant, industrial proletariat. Politically, anarchism arose during this First Wave period in response to the insufficiencies, authoritarianism, and reformism of both radical republicanism and Marxist socialism, and as an organised, mass-based corrective to the vanguard adventurism of *narodnik*[36] populist terrorism.

The Paris Commune of 1871 was a dramatic, innovative, two-month-long popular insurrection, in which several Proudhonists, alongside Blanquists[37] and others, ruled the city after the bourgeoisie fled from their guilt over initiating the disastrous Franco-Prussian War. Although the Commune was not an anarchist affair, its salient feature, that of workers' control of the city, was anticipated by the earlier, short-lived Bakuninist uprisings in Lyons and Marseilles. The fall of Paris and the murder of

approximately 20,000 Communards by the reactionaries
resulted in the First Wave break, the driving underground
of most European revolutionary organisations, and the
subsequent split of the First International into an anarchist majority—based on the massed strength of the First
Wave syndicalist unions—which survived until 1877, as
well as a tiny, short-lived Marxist rump of perhaps only
1,000 adherents, which dissolved in practice after only a
year. The defeat also saw a huge Communard Diaspora
radiate out from France and settle in Belgium, Britain,
Spain, Italy, the United States, and French-speaking
Québec, where they often had a significant radicalising
influence on the nascent working class organisations and
where many of them turned to anarchism/syndicalism.
Meanwhile, the Spanish anarchists gained valuable experience, as the 60,000–strong, anarcho-syndicalist Spanish Regional Workers' Federation (FORE) ran its own
"communes" in the southern cities of Granada, Seville,
Málagar, Alcoy, and San Lucar de Barramed, and co-op-
erated on local communes with federalist "intransigents"
in Grenada, Seville, and Valencia, during the Cantonalist
Revolt of 1873–1874.[38] While the experience with these
communes grounded all future, large-scale, anarchist revolutionary projects, the early "social cantonalist" model
was a narrow one, focused on the FORE's defence and
provisioning of single cities, with no overarching revolutionary plan. There were, nonetheless, significant levels
of social change, including measures of land reform and
wealth taxation, and large-scale peasant mobilisations,
including land seizures.

  Meanwhile, insurrectionist strategies and tactics
were tested by armed anarchist uprisings against the
newly consolidated Italian state in 1874 and 1877 and

they failed because of their lack of social support. The final collapse of the anarchist wing of the IWMA in 1877 ended the first genuinely international attempt to organise the socially-conscious working class, although its torch was soon taken up by the Anti-Authoritarian International (AAI) or "Black International," founded by the likes of Pyotr Kropotkin[39] in 1881, the year of the assassination of Tsar Alexander II by *narodniks*. Pyotr Kropotkin (1842–1921), was a Russian prince, poly-math geographer, zoologist, economist, and evolutionary theorist who turned his back on privilege to become Bakunin's ideological heir and champion of anarchism. Kropotkin's *The Great French Revolution, 1789–1793* (1909) is the definitive libertarian communist analysis, while his books *The Conquest of Bread* (1892), *Mutual Aid: A Factor of Evolution* (1902), and *Fields, Factories and Workshops* (1912) remain among the most accessible and widely read anarchist texts. The Black International included the anarcho- and revolutionary syndicalists of the CGO and the body that merged with it, the Mexican Workers' Grand Circle (CGOM), representing the majority of organised workers in Mexico by 1880, and the Central Labor Union (CLU) in Chicago. The Black International, however, later took an increasingly purist stance, became dominated by the minority anarcho-insurrectionist tendency, and only lasted until about 1893. More generally, the radical working class movement entered a period of defeat that saw an anarchist retreat from mass organisation, while terrorism became vogue for all revolutionary tendencies, and capitalism contracted with two great depressions, the last in 1893. The Black International cultivated an attitude of dangerous clandestinity and, although the American

CLU, for example, continued to operate until 1909, it is primarily remembered today for the 1886 state murder of the Haymarket Martyrs, its militants who are recalled worldwide each year during the commemoration of May Day.[40]

THE BAKUNINIST RESPONSE: THE "INVISIBLE PILOTS" STEER THE SECRET REVOLUTIONARY ORGANISATION

In 1868, Bakunin wrote his seminal work, *Programme and Object of the Secret Revolutionary Organisation of the International Brotherhood*.[41] He laid out the ground-rules for the International Brotherhood (IB) founded that year. The *Programme* reflected Bakunin's rejection of an authoritarian statist solution to the social revolution, "revolutionary in the Jacobin sense," as he put it, an indication of rising tensions between anarchists and Marxists in the IWMA at that time. After spelling out the principles of the anarchist revolution, the *Programme* went on to address organisational matters following the dissolution of the nation-state and its armed forces, bureaucracy, courts, clergy, and private property. Anticipating the anarcho-syndicalist replacement of the state with a decentralised administration of material production and consumption, the *Programme* said that all church and state properties would be put at the disposal of the "federated Alliance of all labour associations, which Alliance will constitute the Commune." A "Revolutionary Communal Council" based on a "federation of standing barricades," comprised of mandated, accountable and revocable delegates from each defensive barricade, would "choose separate executive committees from among its membership for each branch of the Commune's revolutionary administration." This administration would be, according to anarchist principles, of public services, not of people. It would be spread by revolutionary propagandists across all old statist boundaries in order to build "the alliance of the world revolution against all reactionaries combined," the organisation of which "precludes any notion of dictatorship and supervisory leadership authority."

The *Programme* discussed the specific role of the anarchist revolutionary organisation in advancing the social revolution:

> But if that revolutionary alliance is to be established and if the revolution is to get the better of the reaction, then, amid the popular anarchy that is to represent the very life-blood and energy of the revolution, an agency must be found to articulate this singularity of thought and of revolutionary action… That agency should be the secret worldwide association of the International Brotherhood. That association starts from the basis that revolutions are never made by individuals, nor even by secret societies. They are, so to speak, self-made, produced by the logic of things, by the trend of events and actions. They are a long time hatching in the deepest recesses of the popular masses' instinctive consciousness, and then they explode, often seeming to have been detonated by trivialities. All that a well-organised [secret] society can do is, first, to play midwife to the revolution by spreading among the masses ideas appropriate to the masses' instincts, and to organise, not the Revolution's army—for the people must at all times be the army—but a sort of revolutionary general staff made up of committed, energetic and intelligent individuals who are above

all else true friends of the people and not presump-
tuous braggarts, with a capacity for acting as inter-
mediaries between the revolutionary idea and the
people's instincts."

So, in the view of the IB, the anarchist revolutionary
organisation is little more than an intermediary, a mid-
wife and an enabler of mass social revolution, but is nevertheless clearly constituted as a distinct organisation,
albeit submerged within the social struggle.

In his *International Revolutionary Society or Brotherhood*, published in 1865,[42] Bakunin had spelled out the
internal dynamics of such an organisation, then in practice only in embryo form, and the duties of members,
following an exhaustive account of the revolutionary's
understanding and practical application of equality. "He
[sic] must understand that an association with a revolutionary purpose must necessarily take the form of a
secret society, and every secret society, for the sake of the
cause it serves and for effectiveness of action, as well as
in the interests of the security of every one of its members, has to be subject to strict discipline, which is in
any case merely the distillation and pure product of the
reciprocal commitment made by all of the membership
to one another, and that, as a result, it is a point of hon-
our and a duty that each of them should abide by it."
This discipline was entered into, Bakunin stressed, by
the "free assent" of the members, whose first duty was to
society and only secondly to the organisation. Bakunin,
who called in one of his letters for anarchists to be "in-
visible pilots in the centre of the popular storm," has
subsequently been much criticised for the clandestine
nature of his plotting, which has been presumed by

some anarchists to be authoritarian because of its secretive operations and requirements of discipline.

In light of such criticism, it must firstly be recognised that repressive conditions required secrecy. Secondly, the discipline of which he wrote was not an externally imposed one, but a self-discipline to freely abide by commonly-agreed-upon commitments. Thirdly, Bakunin's IB had the practical result of helping to generate the first anarchist, mass-based, revolutionary organisations among the working class, from Spain to Uruguay: namely, the anarcho-syndicalist unions. In 1877, influenced by Bakunin's arguments, a German-language Anarcho-Communist Party (AKP) was founded in Berne, Switzerland, one of the first of scores of specific, self-identified anarchist/syndicalist organisations around the world. The key question raised by Bakunin, that of the role of specific anarchist/syndicalist political organisations, was to remain at the centre of a core debate within the anarchist/syndicalist movement over the ensuing 150 years.

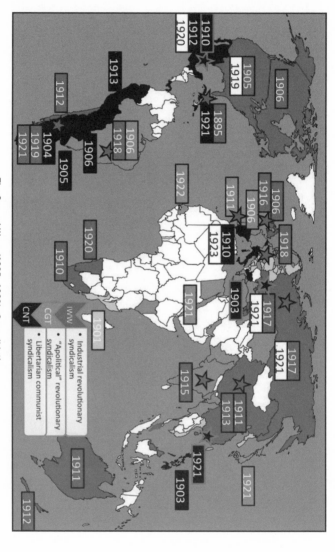

The Second Wave (1895–1923): Consolidation

Legend:
- Industrial revolutionary syndicalism — IWW
- "Apolitical" revolutionary syndicalism — CGT
- Libertarian communist syndicalism — CNT

THE SECOND WAVE, 1895–1923

CONSOLIDATION OF SYNDICALISM AND
SPECIFIC ANARCHIST ORGANISATION IN
A TIME OF WAR AND REACTION

Capitalism began expanding dramatically in the mid-1890s, with the opening up of the African colonies and significant parts of Asia to imperialist exploitation, and a Second Wave of anarcho- and revolutionary syndicalist organising, larger than the first, exploded on to the world scene. An oft-forgotten precursor to this resurgence was the National Labour Secretariat (NAS) of the Netherlands, founded in 1893, which dominated the Dutch labour movement for a decade and peaked at about 18,700 members in 1895. In 1905, a Federation of Freedom-loving Communists (FVC)—later renamed the Country-wide Federation of Freedom-loving

Communists (LFVC)—was founded in the Netherlands, and worked alongside the NAS, but the syndicalists were forced by the state's move towards an early version of the welfare state to cede ground to the moderate Netherlands Union of Trade Unions (NVV). The NAS experienced somewhat of a revival in 1919–1922 with a membership of 30,000 climbing to 51,000—before Bolshevik competition eclipsed it. This Second Wave expansion took two primary forms: anarcho-syndicalism which explicitly recognised its anarchist roots established itself across much of Latin America; and revolutionary syndicalism which obscured its roots, spread across much of the English-speaking world.

Latin American anarcho-syndicalism was largely modelled on, but was a more explicitly anarchist version of, the General Confederation of Labour (CGT) of France, established in 1895. The model proved attractive because anarchist militants of the Federation of Labour Exchanges (FBT)—a horizontal network of labour hiring halls and worker social centres founded in 1892, spreading across France and into French-colonised Algeria and French West Africa, that often survived until independence in the 1960s[43]—had established the CGT by merger in 1902 with the primary union centre, the National Federation of Trade Unions (FNS), meaning that the CGT was based on the local democracy of its FBT sections. In France, this powerful and worker-responsive bottom-up structure had lead to a dramatic growth, with the CGT boasting of 203,000 dues-paying members by 1906. Especially influential was its ringing *Charter of Amiens* (1906), which famously declared that the "trade union, today a fighting organisation, will in the future be an organisation for production and distribution and the basis of social reorganisation." However, the CGT was expressly "apolitical," a weakness that would later allow Marxists and other reformists to hijack it.[44]

This growth was accelerated by two other "jolts" that recalled the direct-democratic practices of the French and Spanish communes, and anticipated the soviets of the Russian Revolution: the 1903 Macedonian Revolt and the 1905–1907 Russian Revolt. In Macedonia, anarchist guerrillas were among those who established communes in Strandzha and Kruševo,[45] while anarchists were involved in establishing the first soviets in Russia, in St. Petersburg and Moscow.[46] The Russian Revolt also saw the establishment in occupied Poland of what is arguably the longest-living, international anarchist organisation, the Anarchist Black Cross (ABC)—originally the Anarchist Red Cross, a splinter off the Political Red Cross—a prisoner's aid network which has member sections in 64 countries today.[47] These jolts helped light the fuse on the formation of the Industrial Workers of the World (IWW) in the USA in 1905, establishing an "industrial revolutionary" syndicalist organising model that swept the Anglophone world in particular, including branches in Australia, Canada, Britain, New Zealand, and South Africa, but also in Argentina, Chile, Cuba, Germany, the Ukraine, Siberia, and elsewhere.[48] The IWW still exists today as a fighting "red" union— although usually as a transverse rank-and-file network across competing unions—with branches in countries as diverse as South Africa and Russia. The IWW *Preamble* was as influential in the Anglophone world as the CGT's *Charter* was in the Hispanophone world, because of the clarity and intransigence of its class politics. According to the *Preamble,*

The working class and the employing class have
nothing in common. There can be no peace so long
as hunger and want are found among millions of
the working people and the few, who make up the
employing class, have all the good things of life. Between these two classes a struggle must go on until
the workers of the world organise as a class, take
possession of the means of production and abolish
the wage system. It is the historic mission of the
working class to do away with capitalism. The army
of production must be organised, not only for everyday struggle with capitalists, but also to carry on
production when capitalism shall have been over-
thrown. By organising industrially we are forming
the structure of the new society within the shell of
the old.

The 1905–1907 Russian Revolt—and especially the
exultation by colonised peoples all over the world at the
spectacle of the defeat of a "white" empire by a "yellow" empire—had a direct impact on the radicalisation
of social struggles in the Far East. Anarchism implanted
itself in Japan from 1906, challenging the second-class
status of both women and the *Burakumin* outcasts who
worked with meat products—and the divine status of
the Emperor. Initially embroiled in attempts to assassinate the Emperor, and bloodily persecuted for supposedly causing the devastating 1923 earthquake, the
movement finally consolidated in 1926 with the formation of the All-Japan Libertarian Federation of Labour Unions (*Zenkoku Jiren*), the third-largest of Japan's
labour federations, after the moderates and the Marxists, which rose to 16,300 members in 1931, when an

explicitly "anarcho-syndicalist" faction, the Libertarian Federal Council of Labour Unions of Japan (*Nihon Jik-yō*) split off, claiming 3,000 members. These numbers exclude the ethnic Korean syndicalist unions in Japan, the various "black societies" (anarchist political groups), and the anarchist tendencies within the *Burakumin* and peasant movements—all of which were suppressed by the fanatically militarised state from 1934 onwards—despite maintaining a twilight presence that survived into the post-war era.[49]

In China, where the movement was first activated in the early 1900s in the Portuguese enclave of Macau (near British-occupied Hong Kong, which became an entry point for IWW ideas) by deported Portuguese anarchists, the nascent anarchist movement threw itself alongside republican forces into the overthrow of the royal dynasty in 1911—the shock of which echoed across Asia. Shifu, the *nom de guerre* of Liu Szu-fu (1884–1915), was the leading Chinese anarchist, who modelled his views on Kropotkin, founded the Society of Anarchist Communist Comrades, and was the pioneer of Chinese syndicalism: the anarcho-syndicalists took the honours of establishing the first modern Chinese trade unions, with the 11,000–strong Teahouse Labour Union in the southern port city of Guangzhou in 1918; Guangzhou would remain an anarchist stronghold for at least a decade after the 1921–1923 period when the entire city was run as an anarchist commune. Further afield in the landmass of China, anarcho-syndicalism initially established itself by 1921 as the majority tendency within the Shanghai-based Confederation of Labour Associations (GLH), which had provincial affiliates as dispersed as the 5,000–strong syndicalist Hunan

Workers' Association (HLH). Black Societies, anarchist schools, and peasant associations flourished, but the flirtations of some leading figures with the heterogeneous *Guomindang* proved fruitless and the movement was suppressed from 1927 as the nationalists consolidated their hold on the cities. By the time the "Maoist" Marxists (Mao having been an anarchist in his youth), defeated the nationalists in 1949, the remaining 10,000 syndicalists had to choose between absorption into the official communist union federation—or exile in reactionary Taiwan.[50]

In Korea, the movement initially arose as a result of radical migrant labour exchanges with Japan, but truly consolidated after the 1910 invasion of the peninsula by Imperial Japan. Despite the proliferation of Black Societies and even of syndicalist trade unions such as the Wonsan General Trade Union and the Free Trade Union in the 1920s, it was in exile across the border in Manchuria that the Korean anarchist excelled. There, in 1929, in a long, mountainous valley, they achieved the least-known anarchist revolution, establishing the Shinmin free zone, based on village direct-democracy and defended by a peasant militia (I will detail this in the Third Wave). When Shinmin was defeated by direct Japanese invasion in 1931, the Korean anarchists fought a long retreat alongside their Chinese comrades, and both guerrilla units and some syndicalist unions survived into the post-war era.[51]

The Russian Revolt also resulted in a London gathering of exiled Russian anarchists, including the anarchist theorists Pyotr Kropotkin, Maria Isidine, and Daniil Novomirsky to discuss an organised response. Maria Isidine, the *nom de plume* of Maria Isidorovna Goldsmith

(1873–1933), was a Russian-French scientist and anarchist, and an advocate of an extreme anti-organisationist—*svobodnikist*—position. Daniil Novomirsky, the *nom de guerre* of Yakob Kirilovsky (1882–193?), the foremost Russian anarcho-syndicalist of his Second Wave generation, was sent to a labour camp in Siberia in 1905, but escaped and settled in New York where he became a prominent pro-organisationist—*burevesnikist*—anarchist journalist. Novomirsky argued that, in order to fight reaction, all "anti-authoritarian socialists should unite into a Workers' Anarchist Party. The next step would be the formation of a vast union of all revolutionary elements under the black flag of the International Workers' Anarchist Party." Such a party required theoretical unity to enable "unity of action." It would be "the only revolutionary party, unlike the conservative parties which seek to preserve the established political and economic order, and the progressive parties [like the Social Democratic Labour Party: both its Menshevik and Bolshevik tendencies] which seek to reform the state in one way or another, so as to reform the corresponding economic relations, for anarchists aim to destroy the state, in order to do away with the established economic order and reconstruct it on new principles." Novomirsky said such a "Party" was "the free union of individuals struggling for a common goal" and as such required "a clear programme and tactics" that were distinct from other currents. It needed to "participate in the revolutionary syndicalist movement [as] the central objective of our work, so that we can make that movement anarchist," and to boycott all state structures, substituting them with "workers' communes with soviets of workers' deputies, acting as industrial committees, at their head."

In 1907, at the International Anarchist Congress in Amsterdam, 80 delegates from Argentina, Austria, Belgium, Bohemia, Britain, Bulgaria, France, Germany, Italy, Japan, the Netherlands, Poland, Russia, Serbia, Switzerland, and the United States met and debated anarcho- and revolutionary syndicalism and the role of specific anarchist/syndicalist organisations.[52] The individualists, who opposed all formal organisation, were roundly defeated by the organisationists, the key resolution being that "anarchy and organisation, far from being incompatible as has sometimes been claimed, are mutually complimentary and illuminate each other, the very precept of anarchy residing in the free organisation of the producers [the syndicalist influenced trade unions]." The congress further hailed the "collective action" and "concerted movement," stating that "[t]he organisation of militant forces would assure propaganda of fresh wings and could not but hasten the penetration of the ideas of federalism and revolution into the working class." The Amsterdam Congress also agreed that labour organisation did not preclude political organisation and urged that "the comrades of every land should place on their agenda the creation of anarchist groups and the federation of existing groups." As a result, participating delegates helped establish a plethora of new anarchist specific organisations. These anarchist federations, some of which were affiliated to the "Amsterdam International," worked in parallel to (and often inside) the anarcho- and revolutionary syndicalist unions. One of the best examples is the Anarchist Communist Alliance (ACA), founded in France in 1911—its descendants in the 2010s are the Anarchist Federation (FA), founded in 1945, and the recent FA splinter the Co-ordination of Anarchist Groups (CGA)—as well as the anarchist Libertarian Communist Organisation (OCL) and Libertarian Alternative (AL).[53]

This powerful shift towards the adoption of Bakuninist-type, specifically anarchist/syndicalist organisations, within the context of mass (including anarcho- and revolutionary syndicalist) organisations and movements, was driven by the likes of the Argentine Regional Workers' Federation (FORA), founded as the country's primary labour centre in 1901, which adopted anarchist-communism as its goal in 1904 and provided the template for similar Second Wave anarcho-syndicalist federations across Latin America, almost all named in echo of the FORA.[54] The FORA totally dominated Argentine organised labour for two decades. It first converted to revolutionary syndicalism its socialist rival, the Argentine Regional Workers' Confederation (CORA), then absorbed it in 1914, leading to the hardline "anarchist-communists" splitting off and forming the FORA of the 5th Congress (FORA-V), and leaving a rump French CGT-styled "apolitical" anarcho-syndicalist FORA of the 9th Congress (FORA-IX), which had peaked at perhaps 120,000 members in 1919. The FORA-IX was absorbed into a new union centre in 1922, which later became Marxist-dominated, but the FORA-V, which peaked at 200,000 members in 1922, reverted to the name FORA and maintained a continuous, if tenuous, presence through decades of dictatorship from 1930, until today. And this is not to mention the MTWIU, which established its Latin American headquarters on the Buenos Aires docks in 1919—or the constellation of specific organisations such as the FORA-IX-affiliated Argentine Libertarian Alliance

(ALA), the FORA-V-affiliated Anarcho-Communist Port-workers' Group (ACAOP), the 5,000–strong autonomous Resistance Society of the Port-workers of the Capital (SROPC), and scores of women's organisations and resistance societies.

Inspired by the FORA, anarcho-syndicalism spread rapidly across the "Southern Cone" of Latin America. The Uruguayan Regional Workers' Organisation (FORU) was founded in 1905, drawing on 40 years of anarchist organisational experience dating back to the anarcho-syndicalist FRROU section of the First International from 1872. The the FORU peaked at 90,000 members in 1911 as Uruguay's dominant labour federation—with a powerful "Feminine Section" (this was *not* a gender ghetto, but rather a vanguard, reflecting the dominance of women in the textile sector which was at the forefront of industrialisation across Latin America; and the Feminine Section model was replicated by all anarcho-syndicalist unions on the continent). Although the FORU's dominance was undercut by an early form of welfare state, and from 1923 by the incursion of Bolshevism into the workers' movement, the movement survived the imposition of dictatorship in 1930 and established an Uruguayan Anarchist Federation (FAU) in 1938 that appears to have survived until 1941—being powerfully revived in 1956.[55]

The Brazilian Regional Workers' Federation (FORB) was founded in Rio in 1906, but within months, it was replaced by a Brazilian Labour Confederation (COB) at national level and a Workers' Federation of Rio de Janeiro (FORJ) at state level. Although revolutionary syndicalism rather than a more explicit anarcho-syndicalism, dominated Brazilian labour during the Second Wave, the sheer size of Brazil meant the COB never achieved true national status and it folded in 1909, being revived between 1913 and 1915. However its constituent regional federations, the FORJ, the Local Federation of Labour of Santos (FOLS), the Workers' Federation of the state of Rio Grande do Sul (FORGS), and the powerful Workers' Federation of São Paulo (FOSP), predated and outlived the COB: the FOSP was still São Paulo state's most important union centre by 1931 under the Getúlio Vargas dictatorship.[56]

In 1905, anarcho-syndicalists formed the Chilean Labourers' Federation (FTCh), which was reformed in 1912 along FORA lines into the Chilean Regional Workers' Federation (FORCh). The FORCh attained a peak of 60,000 members by 1921—but operated alongside the Chilean IWW which was a significant labour centre in its own right with 25,000 members by 1920.[57] The Paraguayan Regional Workers' Organisation (FOR-Pa), founded in 1906, was absorbed in 1916 as the Paraguayan Regional Workers' Centre (CORP), Paraguay's main labour federation, but which in the 1920s lost ground to the Marxists. In 1928, Paraguayan anarchists established among the peasantry a Nationalist Revolutionary Alliance (ANR) the objective of which was "to establish Paraguay as a Communal Republic, part, ultimately, of a 'Federal Union of the Peoples of Latin America.'" But an anarchist insurrection in 1931 was crushed and the unions outlawed, so syndicalists played a role in the underground Workers' Trade Union Reorganisation Council (CORS) until all resistance was suppressed by a joint Marxist and fascist coup in 1936 which laid the groundwork for the pro-Nazi dictatorship of Higinio Morínigo in 1940.[58]

On the Caribbean Rim, the Havana Labour Federation (FOH) was a reformation in 1921 of the moribund Cuban Workers' Confederation (CTC), founded in 1895, and was a forerunner of the Cuban National Labour Confederation (CNOC) which was founded in 1925 on Spanish CNT lines with 200,000 members, Cuba's main labour federation.[59] The Mexican Regional Workers' Organisation (FORM) was a reorganisation in 1915 of the House of the World Worker (COM), founded in 1912 but with a resilient organisational heritage stretching back to the 1860s, Mexico's main labour federation with 150,000 members, and rebuilt as the General Confederation of Labour (CGT) in 1921, which broke apart a decade later.[60] In the late Third Wave, the Venezuelan Regional Workers' Federation (FORV) was formed—I will address this later.

In the Andes, the Peruvian Regional Workers' Federation (FORPe), founded in 1913, was replaced in 1918 with the Local Workers' Federation of Lima (FOL), which became Peru's dominant labour federation.[61] The Colombian Workers' Federation (FOC) was founded in 1925 as the national Colombian trade union central.[62] In Bolivia, the Local Workers' Federation (FOL) of La Paz was founded in 1927 as the reformation of a body founded in 1908, and in the same year, established its formidable Feminine Workers' Federation (FOF). The FOL was reformed in 1930 on FORA lines as the Bolivian Regional Workers' Confederation (CORB). Although the CORB was suppressed by dictatorship in 1936, its FOL/FOF core survived, the latter until 1964.[63] In Ecuador, the Guayas Workers' Regional Federation (FORG) was established by 1928 by the anarcho-syndicalist current in the 30,000–strong Ecuadoran Regional Federation of

Labour (FTRE), founded in 1922. The FORG was suppressed by dictatorship in 1934.[64]

On the Iberian Peninsula, the movement matured with the formation of Spain's massive National Confederation of Labour (CNT), founded in 1910,[65] and the relatively larger National Workers' Union (UON) of Portugal, founded in 1914.[66] The CNT was a revival of a long line of Spanish anarcho-syndicalist labour federations, stretching back to the "grandmother" of them all, the FRE founded in 1868, and rose to 2 million members in 1936. The UON, founded in 1914 with 50,000 members, changed its name to the General Confederation of Labour (CGT) in 1919 when it peaked at 90,000 members, but was suppressed in 1926 by the militarist regime that survived until the "Carnation Revolution" of 1974—which had a devastating effect on anarchist organisations in the Portuguese sphere of influence, such as Mozambique (where an anarchist Revolutionary League had been established in the early 1900s).

In 1910, the first great anarchist-influenced revolution broke out in Mexico, providing the template to be replicated in other upheavals, as to how anarchist-specific organisations, anarcho- and revolutionary syndicalist unions, and armed worker-peasant militia could work in parallel, and sometimes in concert: in the north, the eastern seaboard oil-fields, and Baja California, the Mexican section of the IWW and the Magónistas of the Mexican Liberal Party (PLM)[67] worked together. Ricardo Flores Magón (1874–1922) was the leading figure behind the PLM, which he turned into an armed insurgent anarchist organisation whose militants initiated the Mexican Revolution in 1910. Living much of his life in exile, he died apparently of diabetes in an American prison. In Mexico City and the the central Mexican states, the anarchists/syndicalists of the Struggle (*Lucha*) group worked with the 50,000–strong anarcho-syndicalist House of the World Worker (COM)—the direct descendant of the First Wave Proletarian Circle—defended by its Red Battalions; while south of the capital in Morelos state, Emiliano Zapata's deeply anarchist-influenced Industrial Union of North and South America (UIANS), defended by its Liberation Army of the South (ELS), based on guerrilla militia of 200 to 300 fighters each, numbering 70,000 in total by 1915. This Mexican Revolution also illustrated how things could go awfully wrong. Despite the fact that the interventionist USA had its imperialist intentions diverted by a 1917 entry into the First World War, the Magónistas in the north failed to link up with the Zapatistas in the south, and the anarcho-syndicalists of the COM dramatically failed their watershed test of class solidarity, with some in the COM leadership breaking ranks with the Zapatista peasantry, and sending COM Red Battalions to fight the ELS, on behalf of the statist Constitutionalists. This class betrayal provoked a massive rupture in the COM, with revolutionaries siding with the Zapatistas in the rural areas and the IWW in the oil fields, and the reformists with the treacherous leadership. In disgust, some of the *Lucha* anarchists, such as Antonio Díaz Soto y Gama (1880–1967), broke with the COM, by then reorganised as the FORM. Originally a middle-class lawyer, Soto y Gama had been jailed for writing against the dictatorship in the PLM newspaper, became involved with the *Lucha* organisation and then the ELS, then backed the Zapatistas. But the fragmented Revolution never consolidated its libertarian zones. It sputtered and finally died after

ten exhausting years, gutted by the Constitutionalists'
ability to divide and rule the working class and peasantry. A disillusioned Soto y Gama founded the libertarian
reformist National Agrarian Party (PNA) in 1920, serv-
ing in parliament until 1928. He later wrote the seminal
work, *The Agrarian Revolution of the South and Emiliano
Zapata, Its Leader*.

The internationalist aspect of this new wave of anar-
cho- and revolutionary syndicalism found expression in
the 1913 Syndicalist Conference in London (the British
syndicalist movement was at its peak, with the Industrial
Syndicalist Education League, ISEL, boasting 150,000
members, while the IWW-influenced Irish Transport &
General Workers' Union, ITGWU, in occupied Ireland,
had some 25,000 members and would peak at 120,000
members in 1917),[68] drawing delegates from trade union federations in Argentina, Brazil, Belgium, Britain,
Cuba, Denmark, France, Germany, Italy, the Netherlands, Spain, and Sweden. American IWW and Russian
observers also attended, while Austria adhered without
representation. The congress established an International
Syndicalist Information Bureau. Although disrupted by
World War I, this conference laid the initial groundwork
for the formation of the International Workers' Association (IWA) in Berlin in 1922. Eric Hobsbawm, a Marxist
historian hostile to anarchism, was forced to admit that
"in 1905–14 the Marxist left had in most countries been
on the fringe of the revolutionary movement [and] the
main body of Marxists had been identified with a de facto non-revolutionary social democracy, while the bulk of
the revolutionary left was anarcho-syndicalist, or at least
much closer to the ideas and the mood of anarcho-syndicalism than to that of classical Marxism."[69]

The most powerful anarchist movement in Eastern Europe was the Bulgarian movement, which rose in the 1870s, blooded itself with its valiant defence of Macedonian freedom from the Ottoman Empire in 1903, and which established its first trade unions in 1910. The Federation of Anarchist-Communists of Bulgaria (FAKB) which was founded in 1919 had branches across the country with youth groups in every large school and was a multifaceted armed force to be reckoned with—the third-largest organisation on the left after the agrarians then the Marxists— by the time it resisted the 1923 fascist coup, an extermination campaign in which perhaps 35,000 leftists were slaughtered. By 1931, the rural syndicalist *Vlassovden* Confederation had 130 sections nationwide, and the urban Anarcho-Syndicalist National Confederation of Labour (ASNKR) embraced 40 unions (excluding the IWA-affiliated Bulgarian Confederation of Autonomous Unions). The movement fought against the 1934 fascist coup, then as an underground force against the Nazi and later the Soviet invasions, and by liberation in 1945, the FAKB newspaper *Rabotnicheska Misal* (*Workers' Thought*) had a circulation of 60,000 (at a time when the communist Bulgarian Worker's Party had only 15,000 members)—before being suppressed by a cynical Marxist-fascist-agrarian alliance.

The Second Wave was not broken on the rocks of the First World War, into which the CGT, now dominated by reformists, was drawn. The imperialist powers had initiated the bloodbath because capital was in steep decline and beset on all sides by a militant working class with a lot of remaining momentum. Despite the scale of the slaughter, the conflict unleashed two other Revolutions—Russia and Ukraine—both of which drank

deeply from the well of working class self-organisation
before the counter-revolution unlatched the guillo-
tine-blade. The events in Russia illustrated the danger of
anarchists withdrawing from the battle into purist ivory
towers, while simultaneously proving Bakunin's predic-
tions about the nature of the dictatorship of the proletariat to be chillingly correct, in stark contrast to the
anarchist-flavoured sovietism of the working class. The
Ukrainian Revolution showed the efficiency of an innovative, armed, anarchist struggle, based on conventional
armed forces using rapid-deployment shock tactics. Out
of the original Makhnovist detachment (the *Chernoye
Sotnia*, a cavalry unit of 500 with machine-gun carts)
arose the Revolutionary Insurgent Army of the Ukraine
(RPAU), which, by December 1919, was just over
110,000 strong, divided into four Corps, consisting of
83,000 infantry, 20,000 cavalry, assault groups, artillery,
reconnaissance, medical, and other detachments, including armoured cars and seven armoured trains, and
was headquartered at Aleksandrovsk, Nikopol, Yeka-
terinoslav, and Crimea, but swept like a storm across
south-eastern Ukraine.[70]

The true innovation, however, was not so much in bat-
tlefield tactics, but in the fact that the RPAU forces were
politically pluralistic volunteers (including anarchists, social revolutionaries, Maximalists, non-party fighters and
even dissident Bolsheviks), who elected their officers and,
most importantly, secured the backing of the populace by
redistributing the landed gentry's estates to the peasants.
The forces also submitted themselves to four Congresses
of Peasants, Workers, and Insurgents, which set the general socio-political direction of the movement. In addition, they were linked, more organically than formally,

to Nestor Makhno's Anarcho-Communist Group (GAK) of Gulai-Polye, to the Alarm Confederation of Anarchist Organisations (Nabat), founded in Khar'kov, Kursk, and other centres in 1918, as well as to directly-democratic urban and rural communes, anarcho-/ revolutionary syndicalist-run factories, and the anarchist Black Guard militia which defended them, as well as the 30,000 revolutionary syndicalist coal-miners of the neighbouring Donetz Basin in the eastern Ukraine organised along IWW lines (it must be stressed that the Donetz Basin was by far the *largest* industrial zone in Europe at that time, putting paid to the notion of the movement as merely a bunch of peasants with pitchforks). Apart from those organisations in the broader Makhnovist movement, which included the Congress of Peasants, Workers, and Insurgents, most of these linkages were fluid and informal. Further afield, insurgent Ukraine was linked to the Russian Revolution via the clandestine network of the Pan-Russian Insurgent Committee of Revolutionary Partisans, based in Moscow, which had branches in Russia, the Ukraine, and Latvia. I presume that insurgent Ukraine maintained links via the Trans-Siberian Railway to the 5,000 to 10,000–strong armed formations of I. P. Novoselov's Anarchist Federation of the Altai (AFA) in south-central Siberia[71] and to the revolutionary syndicalist coal-miners of the Kuzbas Basin's 16,000–strong IWW section in Siberia, founded in 1919, which appears to have survived as part of the IWW-dominated "Autonomous Industrial Commune" until being shut down by Stalin's regime as an anomaly in a command economy in 1928. The now-familiar fluid mixture of syndicalist unions, specific anarchist "political" organisations, anarchist militia, and popular communes was replicated in European Russia itself, albeit on a smaller scale: the increasingly beleaguered All-Russian Confederation of Anarcho-Syndicalists (ARKAS), which claimed 88,000 members in 1918, was linked on the factory floor in the Petrograd working class district of Vyborg on the east bank of the Neva River to organisations such as Iosif Bleikhman's Petrograd Anarchist Communist Federation (PACF). In Moscow, the Union of Anarcho-Syndicalist Propaganda (UASP), and the Moscow Federation of Anarchist Groups (MFAG) were linked to the force of 1,000 Black Guards who defended the factories, and the nuclei of pluralistic popular communes were discernible at the anarchist-occupied Villa Durnova in Moscow and more so at the soviet at the Kronstadt naval base located on an island which guarded the Baltic Sea approaches to Petrograd.

While the self-described anarchist/syndicalist movement in Russia, barring the critical exception of the PACF and the anarchist tendency within the Kronstadt Soviet, failed to grasp the bull of power by the horns— in part because they never managed to achieve critical mass among the popular classes as in the Ukraine, the Makhnovist strategy of combining flexible military daring with a libertarian praxis of pluralistic internal democracy, and submitting the whole to civilian plenums, thereby liberating (for a time at least) a shifting territory with some 7 million inhabitants, made the Ukrainian Revolution the most *holistic* of the anarchist social experiments, despite the dire and continually-shifting circumstances of the war, which prevented it from achieving the *continuity* of the later Spanish Revolution. Both the Ukrainian and Russian Revolutions, defended so bravely by the anarchist forces from the assaults of the imperialists, indigenous nationalists, and pro-monarchist Whites, were mercilessly put down by the Bolsheviks. By the time the Global Revolt finally collapsed, with the last gasp of the failed 1918–1923 German Revolution, during which libertarian councillist praxis—the Munich Soviet in particular—had been tested and found wanting, the world was a totally changed place. The First World War and the Spanish Influenza epidemic had wiped out an entire generation, the Conservative counter-revolution was in full swing, the Chinese, German, Austro-Hungarian and Ottoman empires had collapsed, and had been replaced by a constellation of fragile nation-states in which right-wing nationalism ran rampant, and technological innovations like steamships, tanks, aircraft, the telephone, and the automobile had shrunk the world. All of this took place while Fascism and statist Marxist "communism" (or, rather, authoritarian state-capitalism) were deluding the working class with false alternatives to capitalism.

And yet, the Second Wave transformed anarchism into a truly global phenomenon, with sizeable mass anarchist organisations fighting the class war from Costa Rica to China, Portugal to Paraguay, and Sweden to South Africa. Furthermore, global anarcho- and revolutionary syndicalism was drawn together in the International Workers' Association (IWA), founded in Berlin in 1922, a reformation of the libertarian wing of the First International, and representing between 1.5 million and 2 million revolutionary workers globally.[72] In 1922, the IWA's largest sections were the Italian Syndicalist Union (USI) with half a million members, the Argentine FORA, with some 200,000 members, the General Confederation of Labour (CGT) of Portugal, with 150,000 members, the Free Workers' Union of Germany (FAUD), with 120,000 members, and the Committee for the Defence of Revolutionary Syndicalism (CDSR) in France, which had taken 100,000 members away from the now irrevocably reformist CGT, which had peaked at 2.5–million members, most of them white-collar workers far removed from the blue-collar origins of the CGT (one of the ironies of this period is that when the CDSR founded the CGT *Unitaire* (CGTU) in 1921 as a revolutionary rival to the CGT, the new federation attracted Senegalese sailors who had abandoned the Marxists in 1919 after a failed strike). Minor anarcho-syndicalist organisations present at the founding of the IWA came from Czechoslovakia, Mexico, Norway, and Sweden, as well as the Chilean IWW (while most other branches of the IWW were closely sympathetic, they never joined the new international).

The movement's most remarkable achievements at this time included the fostering of a deeply-entrenched tradition of rank-and-file labour militancy and a global proletarian counter-culture that eschewed bourgeois patronage, the establishment of near-universal labour protections, such as the eight-hour working day and worker's compensation, a substantial contribution to the virtual annihilation of absolute monarchism, and the mounting of the most serious challenge to clerical control of education across the world. The defeats of the Mexican, Russian and Ukrainian revolutions did, however, lead a lot of anarchists to become defeatist, withdrawing from the fields of social and industrial struggle they had dominated for decades, leaving the door open to Bolshevism. Those critical of this retreat found themselves having to defend the core principles of the social revolution.

THE PLATFORMIST RESPONSE: THE "GENERAL UNION"
BUILDS AN ORGANISATIONAL PLATFORM

Following their defeat at the hands of the Red Army
whose flanks they had protected for so many years,
Nestor Makhno and many surviving Ukrainian anarchist guerrillas fled into exile in 1921 (a Makhnovist underground would operate in the USSR into the 1930s),
where they faced some hard questions. The most important question was: if anarchism places so much value on freedom from coercion, is it a powerful enough
strategy to defeat a united, militarised enemy? The sur-
vivors were not only embittered by their experiences at
the hands of the "revolutionary" Reds, they were also
greatly disappointed in the poor support they received
from Russian anarchist comrades. Sure, the Nabat had
worked on an ad-hoc basis alongside the RPAU, the anarcho-syndicalist unions in the cities, and the various
Black Guard detachments of guerrillas like Maroussia
Nikiforova, but precious little aid had come from anarchists further afield—and the majority of the Nabat
had split with the RPAU in 1919 over the latter's third
tactical truce with the Bolsheviks.

This dispute over strategy was to play itself out in
exile in France, between ex-Nabatists like Voline and
ex-Makhnovists like Makhno. In 1926, Makhno, Arshinov, Ida Mett, and other exiles from the Workers' Cause
(*Dielo Truda*) group in Paris published a pamphlet entitled *Organizatsionnaia Platforma Vseobshchego Soiuza
Anarkhistov: Proekt* (*Organisational Platform of the General Union of Anarchists: Draft*) or, more simply, the *Platform.*[73] Ida Mett (1901–1973) was a Russian anarchist
who escaped Bolshevik detention, becoming a writer
in exile in Paris; her analysis *The Kronstadt Commune*

(1948) remains a devastating critique of *Bolshevism*. The text caused big waves in the international anarchist movement because of its call for tight internal discipline, mutually agreed upon unity of ideas and tactics, and the formation of a "general union of anarchists." By union, the writers of the *Platform* meant a united specific organisation of tendency, rather than a trade union. They supported anarcho- and revolutionary syndicalism, but stressed that it was "only one of the forms of revolutionary class struggle." Moreover, countering the notion that anarchist/syndicalist unions were self-sufficient, they stressed dual organisationism: unions needed to be united with anarchist political groups, anarchist militias, and anarchist municipal soviets. The *Platform* emphasised the class struggle nature of anarchism, reminding militants that it was a popular class movement, of both the peasantry and the working class, but one that was not exclusively focused on either industry or the trade unions. It called for ideological and tactical unity, collective responsibility, and a programme of revolutionary action. More controversially, it called for an "executive committee" to be formed within the general union of anarchists. By executive committee, the writers of the *Platform* meant a working group of activists, whose job it was to carry out tasks mandated by the union.

The *Platform*'s vision of the future social revolutionary soviet society was arguably derived from an earlier Makhnovist document, the *Draft Declaration of the (Makhnovist) Revolutionary Insurgent Army of the Ukraine*, adopted in 1919 at a congress of the Military-Revolutionary Soviet (VRS), the representative insurgents' body that linked the RPAU General Staff (*Shtarm*), which ran military operations, to the Congresses of Peasants,

Workers and Insurgents. The *Declaration* called, as the Kronstadt Soviet would in 1921, for a "third revolution" against Bolshevik coercive power over the working class, poor, and peasantry, and stated that the basis of this revolution was the free soviet system, "libertarian organisation as taken up by significant masses," freely self-organised to oppose "the notion of political power." However, since the soviets and the RPAU were pluralistic organisations, consisting of anarchists, Social Revolutionaries, and other tendencies, including unaffiliated members, the *Declaration* did not assign the anarchists a specific social function by name. Instead, it stated that not only all "political activity" based on privilege, coercion, and enslavement, but all political organisation, presumably including all genuine socialist revolutionary factions like the anarchists/syndicalists, would "tend to wither away of themselves" under revolutionary conditions.

The *Declaration* further emphasised that the RPAU, while pluralistic, volunteer, and working class-controlled, did form the "fighting core of this Ukrainian people's revolutionary movement, a core whose task consists everywhere of organising insurgent forces and helping insurgent toilers in their struggle against all abuse of power and capital." The militant minority's task was clearly pro-organisational, in support of the popular revolutionary forces. The document, however, stopped short of calling for a specific organisation of a distinct revolutionary tendency to carry out that task, a call the *Platform* later issued. Unlike the central committee of an authoritarian socialist organisation, which would typically make all policy decisions, the *Declaration* stated that the entire membership would form the decision-making body in a platformist organisation. Delegates or committees would merely carry out tasks mandated by that membership. The *Platform* was a restatement of the positions held by numerous anarchist political organisations in previous years, dating back to Bakunin's Alliance. Yet now, some anarchists eschewed the classical Bakuninist line, and put forward unfounded claims that anarchism was traditionally *opposed* to solid anarchist political organisations with a clear political line.

The *Platform*'s critics included veteran anarchist militants such as Voline of Russia, himself a former Nabat member, Sébastian Faure of France, Errico Malatesta of Italy, and Alexander Berkman of the USA. Sébastian Faure (1858–1942) was an influential French anarchist writer, journalist, and radical educator. Errico Malatesta (1853–1932) was a diminutive mechanic and inveterate organiser, widely seen as the leading anarchist theorist after Kropotkin. Spending much of his life in exile, he moved from staging insurrections in Italy to founding anarcho-syndicalist unions in Argentina. Mistakenly hailed as the "Italian Lenin" on his return to Italy, he helped establish the Italian Syndicalist Union (USI) and died under house arrest in the Fascist era. Critics also accused exiles of trying to "Bolshevise anarchism," substituting professional revolutionary elites for the revolutionary masses. The subsequent and much-derided "conversion" of Arshinov to Bolshevism—which was merely a tactical move to enable the exhausted militant to return home—gave the critics lots of ammunition, despite the fact that he was executed in 1937 during Joseph Stalin's purges for allegedly, according to the secret police, "attempting to restore anarchism in Russia."

In 1928, Faure published a response to the *Platform*, *La Synthèse anarchiste* (*The Anarchist Synthesis*), which rejected the arguments of the Platform in favour of a looser ideological mix, which he contended was more in keeping with libertarian free thought; it is from his response that this all-in approach acquired the label "synthesist," with the opposing view termed "platformist." The two tendencies would continue to divide the anarchist movement ever after. Malatesta later conceded that there was no substantial difference between his pro-organisational views, expressed at the 1907 Amsterdam Congress, and those of the Makhnovists; this change of heart was to have a profound impact on the development of platformism in Latin America, where it was termed "specificity" (*especifismo*). Makhno and his co-authors argued that it was exactly because of the disorganisation of Russian anarchists that many of them went on to join the only group with a clear revolutionary plan—the Bolsheviks. Anarchists, they said, needed to be just as clear and as organised, but along libertarian, and not authoritarian, lines and guiding, not dictating revolutionary workers' aspirations. Most of the anarchist opposition to the *Platform* has sprung from misconceptions.

Importantly, its original title as a "Draft" shows that the *Platform* was intended as an internal discussion document within the international anarchist movement, not as a final blueprint for the only possible style of anarchist organisation. It was neither authoritarian (as we have seen in discussing the executive committee), nor was it vanguardist, an attempt to get a tiny group of activists to lead the working class. The intention of the *Platform* was not to suggest that all anarchists should be absorbed into one massive, monolithic "platformist" organisation. It quite clearly stated that platformist groups would maintain links with other revolutionary organisations. The platformist method of organising was applied to all forms of anarchist/syndicalist organisation, whether economic, political, military, or social. Most importantly, the *Platform* was not an innovation, but a clear *re-statement* of the fundamentals of mass anarchist/syndicalist organising, dating back to Bakunin's time. It spoke to the necessity for commonly agreed upon lines of attack, along which anarchist organisations had become the primary promoters of exclusively working class interests worldwide. It was in fact the *Platform*'s harshest critics, such as Voline, who tried to revise anarchism by making a principle of loose organisation without solid politics, an approach that would have made Bakunin turn in his grave.

The intense debate over the *Platform* split the Russian and Ukrainian anarchist movements in exile, notably in France, where the Group of Russian Anarchists Abroad (GRAZ) fractured in 1927 into platformist and synthesist tendencies, and in North America, where the Russian/Ukrainian diaspora likewise split into *burevestnikist* (organisationist) and *svobodnikist* (anti-organisationist) groupings. That year, the platformist tendency in France founded a short-lived International Anarchist Communist Federation (IACF), with sections in France and Italy and delegates from China, Poland, and Spain. The IACF can be considered the ideological descendant of Bakunin's IB and, to a lesser extent, of the organisational Amsterdam Anarchist International, but it never made much headway. In Bulgaria, the platformist tendency proved strongest within the Federation of Anarchist Communists of Bulgaria (FAKB), which adopted the document as its constitution. This may account, in part, for the diversity and resilience of the Bulgarian

anarchist movement, which organised workers, peasants, students, professionals, and intellectuals, and not
only survived, under arms, the 1923 and 1934 fascist
putsches, but also the Second World War, only to be
crushed by Marxist-fascist-agrarian reaction in 1948.[74]
It was unfortunate that the *Platform* was not translated
into Spanish early enough to influence the Iberian Anarchist Federation (FAI). The FAI, founded in 1927, was
envisaged as an Iberian Peninsular organisation embracing Spanish and Portuguese anarchist groups, although
the suppression of the anarchists in Portugal under Sala-
zar made this difficult. It initially rescued the CNT from
reformism, but its lack of internal ideological coherence
allowed it to be hijacked in 1934 by technocrats who
took it into the Catalan regional then Spanish national governments during the Revolution and were on the
verge of transforming it into a conventional political
party when the Revolution was defeated. It has several
active descendants today, all claiming the FAI moniker;
they reject reformism, but remain synthesist.

The debate also influenced those anarchists remaining in Russia itself, including former militants of the
Nabat who had either been driven underground or
jailed. According to a Nabat veteran (unnamed for security reasons), then in exile in Siberia, who wrote in
Dielo Truda in 1928, the Nabat itself, initially a de facto
"synthesist" organisation, had been refining its organisational structure, in the "whirlwind of revolution," in
what approximated a "platformist" direction. The Nabat
veteran wrote that the organisation was, in a sense, a
"party," in that it was not a loose, affinity-based organisation, as claimed by Voline. Rather, they wrote, the
organisation was a federation of groups that rallied "the

most determined, the most dynamic militants with an eye to launching a healthy, well-structured movement with the prospect of a standardised programme." Nabat members submitted to majority decisions reached at its congresses, which transcended its different tendencies to promote a unitary "policy line"—"a single, coherent platform… In short, it was a well-structured, well-disciplined movement with a leading echelon appointed and monitored by the rank and file. And let there be no illusions as to the role of that echelon [later referred to as the 'Secretariat', echoing the *Platform*'s 'executive committee']: it was not merely technically executive, as it is commonly regarded. It was also the movement's ideological pilot core, looking after publishing operations, and propaganda activity, utilising the central funds and above all controlling and deploying the movement's resources and militants."

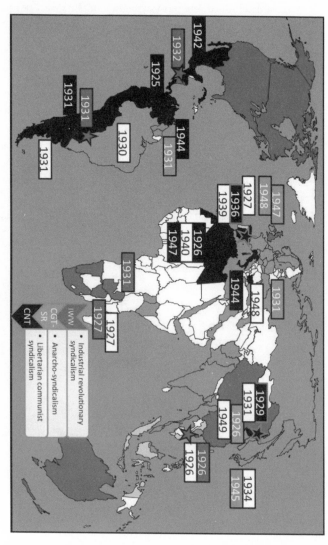

The Third Wave (1924–1949): Expansion

THE THIRD WAVE, 1924–1949

THE ANARCHIST REVOLUTIONS AGAINST
IMPERIALISM, FASCISM, AND BOLSHEVISM

The Conservative counter-revolution of the 1920s generated anarchism's greatest challenge, that of two opposing totalitarianisms, Fascism and Bolshevism, which would crush the autonomous, militant working class in a deadly vise for decades to come. Bolshevism was in many ways more insidious than Fascism, establishing a similar style of totalitarianism, but posing as the liberator of the working class under the "dictatorship of the proletariat" (an early Marxist idea coined by former Prussian military officer Joseph Weydemeyer and expanded on by Marx and Engels). In Russia, the dictatorship's class structure was cynically revealed when Bolshevik leader Leon Trotsky explicitly demanded the regimentation of labour. Disoriented by the propagandist success of the Bolshevik model and silenced in its gulags, anarchism lost ground throughout the world. It did retain strongholds in Latin America and the Far East, while in Brazil, China, Egypt, France, Mexico, Portugal, and South Africa, anarchists helped establish the first "communist" parties, which were initially noticeably anarchist and syndicalist in orientation or, at least, deeply influenced by anarchism/syndicalism until they were Bolshevised on Moscow's orders. It was, however, an era not solely about repression: the Second Wave broke against reformism, the new welfare state sugar-coating that defused militancy in countries as diverse as Uruguay, Sweden, and the USA. While many anarchist/syndicalist organisations were forced underground or destroyed in this long slide into darkness, important struggles against fascism and imperialism were unfolding in countries such as Bulgaria, Korea, and Poland.

In Poland, the anarchist movement had first consolidated during the Russian imperialist period in 1907 with the formation of the Federation of Anarchist-communist Groups of Poland and Lithuania (FAGPL), which operated clandestinely—yet several of its militants were executed by the Russian authorities for belonging to the organisation. A new generation established the Anarchist Federation of Poland (AFP) in 1926 in independent Poland, and before long, a syndicalist General Workers' Federation (GFP) of about 40,000 members emerged. But in the same year, Poland and Lithuania fell under the dictatorship of the socialist ultra-nationalist Jozef Pilsudski, who in 1930 forcibly merged the GFP with nationalist, independent, and socialist unions to form the Union of Trade Unions (ZZZ) as as a yellow union

affiliated to his regime—an odd mix of socialists, liber-
als, and right-wing ex-soldiers—albeit structured along
the lines of the reformist syndicalist French CGT). But
the ZZZ grew to 170,000 members and became dominated by the syndicalists who aligned as a tendency to
the IWA. When the inevitable clash with their employers and the state came, the conservative unions in the
ZZZ such as the munitions workers broke away, leaving
the remainder to be radicalised by the anarcho-syndicalists. The ZZZ was forced underground by the Nazi
invasion in 1939 but reformed as the clandestine Polish
Syndicalist Union (ZSP) with perhaps 4,000 members,
and was active in the underground resistance to Nazism,
publishing papers, cooperating with the Home Army,
and, though its contribution is seldom recognised today, participating directly in the 1944 Warsaw Uprising
through bodies like the 104th Syndicalist company.[75]

It is also worth sketching briefly the trajectories of
the two movements who, more than most, would be
tested in the fires of fascism: those of the Italians and
of the Germans. The Italian movement was born in the
nationalist *Risorgimento*, which united the scattered Italian principalities in 1861, and a section of Bakunin's
Brotherhood was set up three years later. The movement
became involved in localised insurrections in 1874 and
1877, which failed, and despite the popularity of the
creed, struggled to establish a national organisation:
their efforts in establishing the Italian Workers' Party
(POI) in 1882 and the Revolutionary Anarchist Socialist Party (PSAR) in 1891 were wasted as the organisations merged, expelled the anarchists and formed the
Italian Socialist Party (PSI); but the syndicalists came
to dominate many of the regional Chambers of Labour

that were combined in 1906 under Marxist PSI auspices into the General Confederation of Italian Workers (CGIL)—the syndicalists were later expelled, but had managed to form a 200,000–supporter rank-and-file network within the unions. In 1912, this network finally formed an anarcho-syndicalist federation, the Italian Syndicalist Union (USI) with 80,000 members.

Having survived World War I, the syndicalist movement grew dramatically during the *Bienno Rosso*, the "two red years" of 1919 and 1920 when perhaps 600,000 workers occupied their factories, with the USI growing to a respectable 800,000–member minority (the Marxist CGIL had 2.15 million members by 1919, while the conservative unions collectively mustered 1.25–million members). In 1919, a hardline Union of Communist Anarchists of Italy (UCAI) was founded, but was absorbed the following year into the less ideologically rigorous Italian Anarchist Union (UAI), which peaked at 20,000 members. In 1921, the UAI urged the creation of a "United Revolutionary Front," bringing together all leftist forces to combat the rising threat of Fascism. But the Marxist PSI had refused to throw the weight of their CGIL unions behind the factory occupations and by the time of the Fascist "March on Rome" in 1922, the left was demoralised and the numbers of organised workers had fallen sharply; by 1927, with Fascism in full swing, veterans of the USI and UAI lived a twilight life in the resistance—but the once-powerful Marxist CGIL meekly dissolved itself when ordered to do so by the Fascists.[76]

The patchwork of German states had only united in 1871, and for the first three decades, the left suffered under severe anti-socialist laws. So it was only in 1901 that the German syndicalist movement had arisen, when the "localist" tendency within the dominant Marxist Social Democratic Party (SPD) unions split from the SPD and organised as the Free Association of German Trade Unions (FvDG). This soon developed in an anarcho-syndicalist direction under the influence of the French CGT, and of indigenous anarchist and anti-party, anti-state socialism. The membership of the FvDG stood at 18,353 in 1901, compared to the 500,000 members of the Free Trade Unions (FG) linked to the SPD. In 1903, groups across the country formed the German Anarchist Federation (AFD), which worked closely with the FvDG; they were the only left-wing revolutionary organisations in the country on the outbreak of World War I, when the AFD transformed itself into the underground Federation of Communist Anarchists of Germany (FKAD).

The FKAD and FvDG emerged from the war with unsullied reputations for resistance to militarism, and in the heady revolutionary days after the collapse of the German monarchy in 1918, the FvDG expanded to over 100,000 members, and was renamed the Free Workers Union of Germany (FAUD), this time concentrated in the industrial Rhineland and Westphalia and dominated by metalworkers and miners. But the FAUD lost ground on the Rühr to the nascent Bolshevik party—and there were significant revolutionary syndicalist movements to contend with too: even though the FAUD rose to 200,000 members by 1922, it never managed to merge with the 300,000 members of the IWW-styled General Workers' Union of Germany (AAUD), nor with the MTWIU's 10,000 members on the docks, nor even with the more radical anti-Bolshevik syndicalist splinter of the AAUD, the General Labour Union—Unity Organisation (AAU-E) which reached 75,000 members by 1922.

This endemic fragmentation of the German left was to prove fatal when the Nazis rose to power in 1933—by which time the FAUD was a shadow of its former self.[77]

Yet it was also amidst this turmoil that, in 1928 and 1929, two huge continental anarchist organisations were founded. Firstly, the East Asian Anarchist Federation (EAAF), with member organisations in China, Japan, Korea, Formosa (Taiwan), Vietnam, and India, was initiated by the Korean Anarchist Federation's Chinese exile section (KAF-C), which also established the Korean Youth Federation in South China (KYFSC) in Shanghai in 1930, with delegates from Korea, Manchuria, Japan, and all over China.[78] Secondly, the American Continental Workingmen's Association (ACAT) was born, a Latin American IWA formation with member organisations in Argentina, Bolivia, Brazil, Chile, Costa Rica, Ecuador, El Salvador, Guatemala, Mexico, Paraguay, Peru, and Uruguay, which held a founding congress that drew about 100 unions from across the continent.[79] Such ongoing anarchist resistance lead to the upsurge of a Third Wave, with the sorely understudied Manchurian Revolution of 1929–1931, the extreme isolation of which limited its impact to Chinese, Japanese, Manchurian, and especially Korean resistance. The Manchurian Revolution was unusual in that it was initially inserted from above, but quickly gained grassroots support because it was based on worker and community self-organisation.[80] It demonstrated how the uplift of the working class through economic autonomy and education could combine seamlessly with a bottom-up system of decision-making and a militant defensive programme. In 1925, Korean anarchists helped form a "People's Government" administration in the Shinmin

Prefecture bordering on Korea, which helped democra-
tise the prefecture. Subsequently, the Korean Anarchist
Federation (KAF) militant Kim Jong-Jin, a close relative of the anarchist-sympathetic Korean Independence
Army general Kim Jao-Jin, whose forces effectively controlled the Shinmin Prefecture, submitted an anarchist
plan to the military command. It advocated the formation of voluntary rural co-operatives, self-managed by
the peasantry, and a comprehensive education system
for all, including adults. After some debate, and input
from Yu Rim (the alias of Ko Baeck Seong), a founder of
the Korean Anarchist Communist Federation (KACF),
the general and his staff accepted the plan, and the anarchists were given the go-ahead for their plan.

In 1929, anarchist delegates from Hailun, Shi-
htowotze in the Chang Kwan Sai Ling Mountains, Si-
nanchen, Milshen, and other centres, also formed the
Korean Anarchist Federation in Manchuria (KAF-M) at
Hailin. The Shinmin Prefecture was transformed into
the Korean People's Association in Manchuria, a regional, libertarian socialist administrative structure, also
known as the General League of Koreans (*Hanjok Chon-
gryong Haphoi*) or HCH, which embraced a liberated
territory of some two million people. This self-managed
structure was comprised of delegates from each area
and district, and organised around departments dealing
with warfare, agriculture, education, finance, propaganda, youth, social health, and general affairs, the latter
including public relations. Delegates at all levels were
ordinary workers and peasants who earned a minimum
wage, had no special privileges, and were subject to
decisions taken by the organs that mandated them, including the co-operatives. Notwithstanding its bizarre

origins from a meeting between the Kims, Yu, and the Army command, the HCH was based on free peasant collectives, mutual aid banks, an extensive primary and secondary schooling system, and a peasant army. The militia was initially drawn from the Army, but increasingly supplemented by fighters trained at local guerrilla schools. Again, we see the Bakuninist strategy of specific organisations, the KAF-M and the KAFC, operating under the aegis of a delegated civilian mass organisation based on free communes, the HCH, and defended by armed militia. In echo of the Zapatistas in the Mexican Revolution, the "Manchurians" operated almost exclusively in rural areas and relatively small towns. In Fukien province, southern China, which was under informal Japanese influence, situated as it is across the Formosa Strait, KAF-C members participated in the Chuan Yung People's Training Centre, an initiative aimed at establishing an autonomous self-rule district in Fukien, emulating Shinmin. They were subsequently involved in attempts to form a peasant militia and rural communes in the area. But to the north, the Manchurian Revolution was destroyed by the Japanese invasion of Manchuria in 1931, and the KAF-M and KACF were forced to fight a rearguard retreat into southern China, where they continued the armed struggle against Imperial Japan alongside their Chinese comrades until Japan's defeat in 1945.

However, it was the explosion of the running class war in Spain into full-throated revolution, taking place when the Fascist-oriented colonial military staged a coup d'état in 1936, that captured the attention of the whole world. Seen as a laboratory of virtually every known competing political tendency from anarchism to Fascism, the Spanish Revolution was in many ways the

most compelling of the century. Detail on the Spanish
Revolution of 1936–1939 is largely unnecessary because
the events are so well known. For my purposes here,
suffice it to say that the loosely-structured Makhnovist
model of free communes and soviets, organically linked
to revolutionary/anarcho-syndicalist unions (IWW,
etc.), overseen by a mass class organisation (Congress
of Peasants, Workers, and Insurgents), linked to specific
anarchist organisations (Nabat, GAK, etc), and defended by affiliated or autonomous militia (RPAU and the
Black Guards) was replicated. It was done in a tighter
formation and a more continuous fashion in the cities
of Catalonia, Aragon, and Valencia than had been the
case in Ukraine, where the constantly shifting front-line
had meant that Makhnovist urban administrations had
few chances to establish themselves for long. The Spanish Revolution saw free communes more closely linked
to the two-million-strong, anarcho-syndicalist National
Confederation of Labour (CNT), which had declared
itself for libertarian communism at its 1936 Zaragoza
Congress. The CNT, in turn, was in formal alliance
with the synthesist Iberian Anarchist Federation (FAI),
the Libertarian Youth Federation of Iberia (FIJL), and
its Catalan-language corollary, the Libertarian Youth
(JJLL). The CNT-FAI-FIJL and the free communes
were defended by affiliated Confederal militia, such as
the famous Durruti Column.[81] Sadly, compromises and
strategic blunders were made by reformists and oppor-
tunists in the anarchist ranks, who betrayed the class line
by elevating the CNT-FAI to regional and then national
office in the Republican state, accepting minority posts
on the Councils of Aragon and Valencia when they were
the overwhelming majority on the ground, and failing

to implement the Zaragoza resolution on establishing a national Defence Council to federate all worker and peasant communes. Equally destructive were the technocrats in the FAI who attempted to turn it into a conventional political party, a seizure of the organisation made possible precisely because of its synthesist lack of internal coherence, and undermined the Revolution from within.[82] Along with the earlier experiences of the handful of leading anarchists in Czechoslovakia, China, and Korea who tried to use the vehicle of the nation to achieve anarchist ends, the example of Spain clearly shows that internationalist anarchism and the interests of the global working class are totally at odds with nationalist government, however "revolutionary." The outside support for the Francoist rebels of the pro-Fascist imperial powers, the betrayals of the Bolsheviks, and the extremely fragmented nature of the republican camp all led to Spain being recalled, incorrectly, as the swan-song of anarchism, a song soon drowned in the carnage of the Second World War. Still, the worker- and peasant-run fields and factories of Spain—the socialised tramways of Barcelona carried eight million passengers annually—provided the best-studied methods for the successful operation of an egalitarian society on a large scale, a lesson that humanity will not easily forget.

Although the defeat of the Manchurian and Spanish Revolutions was a great blow for the class, the Third Wave did not break until the end of the Second World War, when it peaked with armed anarchist resistance movements in France, China, Korea, Poland, Italy, Bulgaria, Hungary, and Francoist Spain, movements that were soon echoed in the anti-colonial struggles to come. Not only that, but numerous anarchist federations were formed in the closing phases of the World War II period and its immediate aftermath, as anarchists attempted to rebuild their political and trade union presence. According to Phillip Ruff, the Nabat was re-established in the Ukraine and staged an armed uprising in 1943, being commended by the 4th Guard of the Soviet Army for holding a bridgehead on the west bank of the Dnieper River. Its leader, school headmaster V.I. Us, was, however, jailed by the Soviet authorities for four years, though rehabilitated after Stalin's death. Ukrainian anarchist partisans reportedly continued fighting as late as 1945, while within the Red Army occupying Germany and Austria immediately after the war, a secret Makhnovist organisation called the Kronstadt Accords (ZK) apparently operated.

In this period, along the lines of the Amsterdam model, anarchist-specific organisations suppressed by the war emerged in parallel to anarcho-/revolutionary syndicalist unions. For example, in France, the clandestine International Revolutionary Syndicalist Federation (FISR) emerged in 1943, leading to the establishment of the National Confederation of Labour (CNT) in 1945, alongside and within which operated the Francophone Anarchist Federation (FAF), which was established the same year. It is possible that the 17,500 Senegalese who defected in 1948 from the French Marxist CGT, joined the anarcho-syndicalist CNT which had a far more progressive stance towards national independence for the colonial world—but I am still researching this. The Federation of Anarchist Communists of Bulgaria (FAKB) and its unions resurfaced. In Italy, the Federation of Italian Anarchist Communists (FdCAI) was founded in 1944 and had some influence on the anarchist tendency in the new General Italian Workers' Federation (CGIL).

The Anarchist Federation of Britain (AFB) was founded in 1945 and worked alongside the new Syndicalist Workers' Federation (SWF). The AFB did not survive the Third Wave, and another regional federation was only rebuilt during the Fourth Wave in 1967, alongside an equally short-lived Anarchist Communist Federation (ACF) the following year. The ACF seeded a lineage in the 1970s, however, which resulted in the refounding of the ACF in 1986.[83]

The Japanese Anarchist Federation (JAF) was founded clandestinely under US military occupation in 1945 with about 200 members, followed the next year by the syndicalist Federation of Free Labour Unions (FFLU) and Conference of Labour Unions (CLU).[84] The JAF split in 1951, with the "pure" anarchists founding the Japanese Anarchist Club (JAC) and the anarcho-syndicalists forming the Anarchist Federation which in 1955 was renamed the JAF again. It affiliated to the IFA but collapsed in 1968, being replaced by the Black Front Society (KSS) in 1970, followed by a Libertarian Socialist Council (LSC). In 1983, the anarcho-syndicalist Workers' Solidarity Movement (RRU) was established, becoming for a while the Japanese section of the IWA. In 1988, a new Anarchist Federation was established in Japan. In 1992, the Workers' Solidarity (RR) anarcho-syndicalist network split from the RRU, which turned towards ultra-left communism and left the IWA.

New formations also emerged in regions where organised anarchism had been absent for some time: the Federation of Libertarian Socialists (FFS) was established in Germany in 1947; built by the likes of veteran anti-militarist, anarcho-syndicalist, and journalist Augustin Souchy (1892–1984)—who was active in Germany, then in exile in Revolutionary Spain, jailed in France, then active in Mexico, and who wrote probably the best first-hand critique of looming authoritarianism in Revolutionary Cuba in 1960—the FFS survived into the 1950s. In 1977, an anarcho-syndicalist Free Workers' Union (FAU) was established in Germany in echo of the old FAUD; still active today, it is affiliated to the IWA and is online at www.fau.org. The North African Libertarian Movement (MLNA), which came to embrace Morocco, Algeria, and Tunisia, was founded in 1947.[85] The revolutionary syndicalist Independent League of Trade Unions (OVB) was founded in the Netherlands in 1948; the OVB, which is online at www.ovbvakbond.nl, was based among dock-workers and fishermen at The Hague, Rotterdam, and Amsterdam; it split in 1988 with the anarcho-syndicalists leaving to form the Free Union (VB), which is online at www.vrijebond.nl. The collapse of Spain also sent an anarchist diaspora out into the world, from North Africa to Chile. Its greatest impact was felt in France, where militants fought in the resistance against the Nazis, in Cuba, where the movement experienced a dramatic growth-spurt, coming to dominate both the "official" and the underground union federations after World War II, and in Mexico and Venezuela where the exile presence was large enough to form two significant autonomous anarcho-syndicalist formations: the General Delegation of the CNT (CNT-DG) in Mexico in 1942, which co-ordinated CNT exile Sub-Delegations across Latin America, and the Venezuelan Regional Workers' Federation (FORV) in 1944.[86]

Another strongpoint of anarcho-syndicalist organising in the immediate post-war period, usually overlooked, may have existed in China, where the movement reportedly maintained a minority trade union presence of only about 10,000–strong in Guangzhou and Shanghai together, under the difficult conditions of conflict between the nationalists and the Bolsheviks, but this is hard to verify. In Korea, the defeat of Japan lead to a rapid reorganisation of anarchist forces, as the KAF-C, its youth wing, the KYFSC, affiliates in the Eastern Anarchist Federation, as well as many other "black societies," combined to create the huge Federation of Free Society Builders (FFSB).[87] A strong libertarian reformist tendency also developed, with the entry of a few key members of the KACF, such as Yu Rim, and of the Korean Revolutionist Federation (KRF), into the five-party, left-wing Korean Provisional Government (formed in exile in 1919) from 1940 until about 1946. American and Russian occupational forces allowed this shadow government no access to power and supplanted it with their own proxy governments in 1948.

In 1948, at a pan-European anarchist conference in Paris, the Anarchist International Relations Commission (CRIA) was established with the aim of maintaining ties between the dispersed, rather battered, but still vibrant, post-war anarchist movement. CRIA established a sister organisation in Latin America, the Montevideo-based Continental Commission of Anarchist Relations (CCRA). The CRIA/CCRA saw itself as continuing the work of the 1907–1915 Amsterdam International and maintained a network of correspondence between anarchist organisations, journals, and individual militants in Algeria, Argentina, Australia, Bolivia, Brazil, Britain, Bulgaria, Canada, Chile, China, Colombia, Cuba, Ecuador, France, Germany, Guatemala, India, Israel, Italy, Japan, Korea, Mexico, Morocco, the Netherlands,

Panama, Peru, Portugal, Spain, Switzerland, Tunisia, Uruguay, the United States, Venezuela, and Yugoslavia. The CRIA/CCRA held its first congress in Paris in 1949, and, at its congress in London in 1958, it joined with the Provisional Secretariat on International Relations (SPIRA) and was transformed into the Anarchist International Commission (CIA), which survived until about 1960.[88]

THE DURRUTIST AND NEO-MAKHNOVIST RESPONSE: THE "REVOLUTIONARY JUNTA" PUSHES FOR A FRESH REVOLUTION

During the Spanish Revolution, at the height of the Third Wave, anarchists faced the same question raised in the 1920s by the Platform: how to organise in a free, yet effective, manner. Aware that the communists and reformists within the trade unions were selling out the revolution, a militant group of anarchists formed in 1937 to maintain the revolutionary hard line. The Friends of Durruti (AD) were named after the brilliant Spanish anarchist railway worker and guerrilla fighter, Buenaventura Durruti, who died defending the capital of Madrid against the Francoist forces in 1936. The AD was founded by rank-and-file CNT militants, key anarchist hardliners, and anarchist militia, in particular from the famous Durruti Column and the Iron Column. They opposed the "revolutionary" state's order to turn the militia into an ordinary authoritarian army, with class divisions and a murderous regime of punishment.

In 1938, encouraged by the Spanish Communist Party, the counter revolution was in full swing, in the rear of and at the revolutionary front. The AD published

Towards a Fresh Revolution, a strategic document that critiqued the reformist tendency within the CNT, one which had lead to confederated collaboration with bourgeois, nationalist, conservative, and Bolshevik forces in the Republican government. The document called for a "revolutionary *junta*" (meaning a "council" or "soviet") to maintain the revolutionary character of the war by means of the anarchist/syndicalist militia, and for the economy to be placed entirely in the hands of the syndicates—the revolutionary anarcho-syndicalist unions which made up the base of the CNT. It was, in effect, a call by the organised revolutionary working class under arms to dissolve the bourgeois Republican government and replace it with a decentralised militant counter-power structure. In the document, the AD also demanded the seizure of all arms and financial reserves by the workers; the total socialisation of the economy and food distribution; a refusal to collaborate with any bourgeois groups; the equalisation of all pay; working class solidarity; and a refusal to sign for peace with foreign bourgeois powers.

Like the Makhnovist *Platform*, the AD manifesto was also labelled vanguardist and authoritarian, this time because of a misunderstanding, mostly among English-speakers, of what was meant by the revolutionary *junta*. In the AD's usage, *junta* did not have the connotations of a ruling military clique that the term carries in English. It was not to be an "anarchist dictatorship," supplanting the bourgeois government with an anarchist one. Its task was merely to co-ordinate the war effort and make sure that the war did not defer or dismantle revolutionary gains. The rest of the revolution was to be left in civilian worker hands.

In 1945, the Bulgarian platformist FAKB, founded in 1919, called a congress at Knegevo, in the capital city of Sofia, to discuss the repression of the anarchist/syndicalist movement by the Fatherland Front government. This government had been installed by the Red Army and consisted of Communist Party and Agrarian Union members and fascist *Zveno* officers, involved in the 1934 fascist putsch. However, all 90 delegates were arrested by Communist militia and put into forced labour camps. Anarchist locals were forcibly shut down and the revived FAKB newspaper *Rabotnicheska Misal* (*Workers' Thought*) was forced to suspend publication after only eight issues. It reappeared briefly during Fatherland Front-rigged elections, held in 1945 under American and British pressure, surging from a circulation of 7,000 to 60,000, before being banned again. More than 1,000 FAKB militants were sent to concentration camps and the next annual congress of the FAKB had to take place clandestinely in 1946.

Despite the repression, in 1945, the FAKB was able to issue a key platformist strategic document. The *Platform of the Federation of Anarchist Communists of Bulgaria* argued for an anarchist/libertarian communist future order. While rejecting the traditional political party as "sterile and ineffective," and "unable to respond to the goals and the immediate tasks and to the interests of the workers," it advocated for anarcho-/revolutionary syndicalist unions, cooperatives, and cultural and special organisations (like those for youth and women), as well as a specifically anarchist political group along the lines of the original 1927 *Platform*:

It is above all necessary for the partisans of anarchist communism to be organised in an anarchist communist ideological organisation. The tasks of these organisations are: to develop, realise and spread anarchist communist ideas; to study the vital present-day questions affecting the daily lives of the working masses and the problems of the social reconstruction; the multifaceted struggle for the defence of our social ideal and the cause of working people; to participate in the creation of groups of workers on the level of production, profession, exchange and consumption, culture and education, and all other organisations that can be useful in the preparation for the social reconstruction; armed participation in every revolutionary insurrection; the preparation for and organisation of these events; the use of every means which can bring on the social revolution. Anarchist communist ideological organisations are absolutely indispensable in the full realisation of anarchist communism both before the revolution and after.

According to this neo-Makhnovist manifesto, such anarchist political/ideological organisations were to be federated across a given territory, "co-ordinated by the federal secretariat"—similar to the Durrutist "revolutionary junta"—but the "local organisation" was to remain the basic policy-making unit, and both local and federal secretariats to be "merely liaison and executive bodies with no power" beyond executing the decisions of the locals or federation of locals. The *FAKB Platform* emphasised the ideological unity of such organisations, stating that only committed anarchist communists could be members, and that decision-making must be by consensus, achieved by both persuasion and practical demonstration, rather than by majority vote (the latter being the method applicable to anarcho-/revolutionary syndicalist and other forms of organisation, with allowances made for dissenting minorities). Anarchist militants, so organised, would participate directly in both syndicalist unions and mainstream unions, arguing their positions, defending the immediate interests of the class, and learning how to control production in preparation for the social revolution. Militants would also participate directly in co-operatives, "bringing to them the spirit of solidarity and of mutual aid against the spirit of the party and bureaucracy"—and in cultural and special-interest organisations which support the anarchist communist idea and the syndicalist organisations. According to the *FAKB Platform*, all such organisations would relate to each other on the basis of "reciprocal dependence" and "ideological communality."

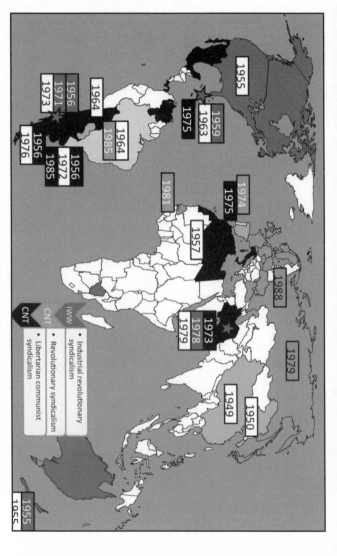

The Fourth Wave (1950–1989): Rearguard

THE FOURTH WAVE, 1950–1989

REARGUARD ACTIONS IN THE SHADOW OF THE COLD WAR AND DECOLONISATION IN AFRICA AND ASIA

The anarchist movement is widely seen as being at its lowest ebb in the 1950s, when capitalism was in a post-war boom, and the Cold War between the alternate capitalisms of the USA and USSR was at its height. To a large extent this is true. In 1955, the IWW was at its weakest in 50 years of existence, neo-fascism was still ascending in most of Latin America and the Mediterranean, Bolshevism was ascending in the Far East, the revolution in China had largely been lost to "Maoist" Marxist totalitarianism in 1949, and Korea was permanently carved into red and white totalitarian camps by 1953, closing the door on both revolutionary anarchist and libertarian reformist options.

This view, however, ignores the key role played in Cuba by anarchists within the Second Escambray Front, the Student Revolutionary Directorate (DRE), the state's Cuban Labour Confederation (CTC), and even *within* Fidel Castro's 26th of July Movement itself.[89] The anarchists had their own organised presence, as well. The Federation of Anarchist Groups of Cuba (FGAC) had been founded in 1924 and reorganised as the Cuban Libertarian Alliance (ALC) in 1939; reconstituted in 1944, during the Cuban Revolution, the ALC had sections in all Cuban provinces, with wide influence in both the cities and in the rural areas, among industrial workers and plantation workers, miners and craft workers, fishermen and journalists, dockers and transport workers. The clandestine anarcho-syndicalist General Confederation of Labour (CGT) had been founded in 1931 under the US-backed Gerardo Machado dictatorship as an underground union federation, taking with it many sections of the formerly anarcho-syndicalist CNOC (founded in 1925) which had been transformed under Marxist leadership into the "yellow" Cuban Labour Confederation (CTC), run by the Batista regime. By a twist of fate, when Fulgencio Batista had been defeated at the polls in 1944 (before his dictatorial return in 1952) and his Marxist allies were kicked out of the leadership of the CTC, the vacuum was filled by the anarcho-syndicalists, meaning that at the time the Revolution erupted, they ran both the underground CGT and the official CTC.

Given that the Cuban Revolution remains, to this day, the touchstone of diverse tendencies arising from the New Left, the centrality of the anarchist movement to the anti-Batista Revolution, and the fraudulent, counter-revolutionary role played by the Castroites who militarised and impoverished Cuban society, destroyed free labour, and corporatised the unions along Fascist lines, building a traditional Latino strong-man personality cult around Fidel Castro, a close friend of Nazi sympathiser Juan Perón of Argentina and of Franco's interior minister Manuel Fraga Iribarne (whose former bodyguard was the leader of the Argentine Anti-Communist Alliance, "Triple-A," death-squad), cannot be overemphasised—but is beyond the scope of this book to detail.[90] Suffice to say that from 1961, when Castro established a USSR-backed populist dictatorship on Perónist/corporatist lines, the CGT was outlawed and many of its members either jailed or driven into exile while the CTC was absorbed into the state.

So the common suggestion that the Swedish Workers' Central Organisation (SAC)[91] was the sole remaining lighthouse of large-scale anarcho-syndicalism, until its withdrawal from the IWA in 1959, not only occludes the experience of the Cuban CGT and CTC, but ignores the fact that the Chilean IWW, the anarcho-syndicalist General Confederation of Labour (CGT), and the anarcho-syndicalist National Workers' Unity Movement (MUNT) of Chile combined to establish the powerful Chilean Workers' Central (CUT) in 1953, along with the Marxist and socialist unions. The CUT's national leadership included nine socialists, four anarchists, two Marxists, two Christian democrats, an independent left-wing Christian, and even a right-wing Phalangist; its statement of aims and principles was, in fact, drawn up by three anarchists. Within the CUT, the anarchists controlled the maritime workers, shoemakers, and printers. The CUT built up membership among students, manual labourers, peasants, intellectuals, and professionals, and started making demands that were political and social, as well as economic. As a result, in 1956, the CUT declared a general strike and shut down the entire country for two days. The Paco Ibáñez regime offered to hand over power to the CUT, but the Marxist and socialist parties agreed to back down and end the strike, against the strong objections of the anarchists. The meddling left-wing politicians had sabotaged the first real chance to establish workers' control in Chile and, in fact, Latin America.[92]

The view that this period saw the end of anarchist organisation also ignores other evidence of anarchist/syndicalist presence: the massive six-month strike by the FORA-led Ship-building Workers' Federation (FTB) in Argentina in 1956, the country's largest strike in the 20th Century; the five-month resistance by some 100,000 syndicalist-influenced workers on the docks, mines, and freezing plants of New Zealand in 1951;[93] the guerrilla campaigns of the 1940s and 1950s in the southern Yunan province of China, near the border with Burma and Vietnam, carried out by the anarchist guerrilla Chu Cha-pei and modelled on those of the Makhnovists and RPAU;[94] the continued anarchist domination of the FOL's successor, the Bolivian Regional Workers' Confederation (CORB) and its powerful Feminine Workers' Federation (FOF) under the leadership of Petronila Infantes, which lasted until 1964;[95] and the survival of the revolutionary syndicalist-influenced Industrial and Commercial Union of Southern Rhodesia (ICU *yase* Rhodesia) into the mid-1950s.[96] Still, it was largely a period of hibernation, in which much of the syndicalism in evidence was "spontaneous" and divorced from its anarchist origins.

That started to change with developments like the founding of the hugely influential Uruguayan Anarchist Federation (FAU) in 1956, an organisation that despite possessing a mere 500 official members built a 10,000–person Worker-Student Resistance (ROE) network and a syndicalist National Convention of Workers (CNT) that was 400,000 strong by 1972, and which set the scene for Latin American continental resistance in the years to come.[97] Despite operating in the most difficult of conditions, anarchist guerrillas plagued the authorities in "Maoist" China and Francoist Spain, while there were reformist libertarian resistance organisations in Allied-occupied South Korea: the clandestine Autonomous Workers' League (AWL) and the Autonomous Village Movement (AVM), both creations of the synthesist FFSB, the latter managing to maintain a twilight existence into the mid-1970s.[98] Still, anarchism, and the working class as a whole, with which it has always been closely associated, was in dire straits. It was only resuscitated on a global scale by the "jolt" of 1968, which initiated a wave of working class resistance to the various forms of capitalism, with youth revolts in Czechoslovakia (bloodily repressed by a Warsaw Pact armed invasion), France (where 10 million striking workers almost toppled the Charles de Gaulle regime), Italy, Japan, Mexico (where the Institutional Revolutionary Party's forces committed the Tlatelolco Massacre in Mexico City against protesters), Pakistan, Poland, Yugoslavia, the US, West Germany, and in the former French colony of Senegal where the National Union of Senegalese Workers (UNTS) came close to seizing control of the state. In the old anarcho-syndicalist stronghold of Hunan province, China, a group called the Federation of the Provincial Proletariat (*Shengwulian*) emerged from the "Red Guards" that broke with both sides of the Chinese Communist Party, and upheld the grassroots, federalist traditions of the Paris Commune of 1871 and the Petrograd Soviet of 1917. The jolt, spurred on by the neoliberal contraction of capital, which started dismantling the West's welfare states and further eroded working class conditions in the Soviet bloc, unleashed a Fourth Wave of anarchist organisation and guerrilla warfare, centred primarily in the southern cone of Latin America, but also in the Middle East, a new field of anarchist operations.

During this wave, anarchism and the libertarian strains of autonomism that sprang up in Western Europe in the 1970s usually played second fiddle to Maoism and Trotskyism, with many Western anarchists influenced by the insurgent doctrines of the authoritarian Marxist rural guerrilla strategist Ché Guevara, rather than by the libertarian communist urban guerrilla strategist Abraham Guillén, whose ideas dominated in the Southern Cone of Latin America among the anarchists and "Trotskyists."[99] In Chile, the armed Movement of the Revolutionary Left (MIR) had an anarchist faction which existed from its founding in 1965 until most of them left in 1967, and its military-political line was laid down by libertarian communist Marcello Ferrada-Noli. Several former MIR guerrillas were later involved in the post-Pinochet founding of the Anarcho-Communist Unification Congress (CUAC), later renamed the Libertarian Communist Organisation (OLC). Explicitly anarchist guerrilla organisations of this period in the global south included the FAU's Revolutionary

Popular Organisation 33 (OPR-33) of Uruguay, powerfully influenced by Guillén's theories, and which defended the FAU-founded syndicalist National Convention
of Workers (CNT), and other class formations during
the Juan Bordaberry dictatorship; and Libertarian Resistance (RL) of Argentina, which defended the factories
during the murderous Rafael Videla dictatorship.[100]

In Iraq, in 1973, the 300–strong Workers' Liberation Group (*Shagila*) split from the Iraqi Communist
Party because of its rapprochement with the quasi-fascist ruling Ba'ath Party—adopted a self-described "anarchist-communism" and waged a bitter campaign against
Ba'athist secret policemen. Shagila's entire membership
illegally crossed into Iran in 1978 to help the indigenous Iranian anarchist movement, The Scream of The
People (CHK), which had splintered off the "Maoist"
splinter of the leftist Fedayeen, support the autonomous
neighbourhood *shorahs* and worker's *kommitehs* of the
genuine Iranian Revolution which ousted the dictatorial Shah, the most recent revolution in which anarchist
guerrillas played a role. The outstanding Polish journalist Ryszard Kapuściński—who personally witnessed 27
revolutions and coups in the "Third World"—was in
Tehran in late 1979, and his book on the causes of the
revolution, *Shah of Shahs*, refers to "opposition combat
groups" including "anarchists" but in contradiction to
his evidence, former Iranian Fedayeen guerrilla turned
anarchist exile "Payman Piedar" claimed in a 2005 interview with me that this description was probably
politically inaccurate. When the Ayatollah Khomeini's
French-backed counter-revolution rolled forward in
mid-1979, most Shagila and CHK members were mas-
sacred, yet both organisations remain important for our

understanding of anarchist praxis in that they developed a form of anarchism virtually in total isolation from the rest of the anarchist movement, giving an indication of the universal validity of revolutionary anarchism.[101]

In the global north, anarchist guerrilla organisations included: the Angry Brigade (AB) of Britain, which focused exclusively on sabotage; Direct Action (AD) of France, members of which later took a "Maoist" Marxist turn; Direct Action (DA) of Canada; the Movement 2 June (M2J) of Germany, several of whose members later joined the Red Army Faction (RAF); and the Anti-capitalist Autonomous Commandos (KAA) of the Basque country. Between 1979 and 1984, eight KAA militants were killed in action, 14 were jailed and others fled into exile in Latin America.[102] An important pole of revolt in Europe in this period was a trio of guerrilla organisations that arose from the Spanish exile MLE's Interior Defence (DI) organisation established in 1961 to assassinate Franco: the First of May Group (GPM) founded in 1965, the Iberian Liberation Movement—Autonomous Combat Groups (MIL-GAC) founded in 1971, and the Groups of International Revolutionary Action (GARI) founded in 1974, which ended its actions only several months before Franco died in 1975.[103]

Other important developments during the Fourth Wave were the re-establishment of the Anarchist Black Cross (ABC) in 1968, initially to deal with the issue of anarchist political prisoners in Francoist Spain, especially those condemned to death by garrotte, and the founding of the synthesist International of Anarchist Federations (IAF) at a congress in Italy the same year. The IAF built on the international network of the CIA, which had become moribund in approximately 1960. It

drew in young militants and older groups, and played
a key role in breaking the pro-Castro sentiment of sec-
tors of the anarchist movement, though it was to lose its
own Cuban section over this question. Its key section at
the time was the FAF in France, but the 1968 congress
drew in regional anarchist organisations from Argentina, Australia, Britain, Bulgaria (the exile Bulgarian Libertarian Union), the Cuban Libertarian Movement in
Exile (MLCE),[104] Italy, Japan, Mexico,[105] Norway, the
Netherlands, Switzerland, and the underground Iberian
Anarchist Federation (FAI) of Spain and Portugal—as
well as anarchist groups in Greece and Germany. In
1971, the IAF held its second congress in Paris under
more difficult circumstances, but reaffirmed its libertarian communist principles. Later, the Cuban MLCE
withdrew in a dispute over the IFA's failure to adopt a
hard line against the Castroist counter-revolution. Of
particular interest are evidence of links with groups in
regions where an anarchist presence would not normally
be expected: a Neutralist Tribune from Vietnam; and an
Anarchist Federation from China, which was perhaps
based in Hong Kong. In the 1970s, in addition to its
member organisations, the IFA had contacts with anarchist federations in Australia, Chile, Denmark, Baden
(Germany), Japan, New Zealand, Portugal, Québec
(Canada), Scotland, Sweden, and the underground
Uruguayan Libertarian Alliance (ALU), the IWA affil-
iate that split from the FAU in 1963.

This mushrooming of anarchist organisations across
the world was matched by the resurgence of anarcho-
and revolutionary syndicalism, as well as autonomous
worker organising that paralleled syndicalism in many
ways, in varied circumstances. For example, there was

the establishment of an IWW Marine Transport Workers' Industrial Union (MTWIU) section in Sweden. One of the key spurs to the resurgence of anarchism was the end of the quasi-fascist regimes in Portugal in 1974, and Spain in 1975, which saw the dramatic re-emergence of the CNT, with a membership of 200,000. In this period, however, the real harbinger of things to come was the re-emergence of anarchism and revolutionary syndicalism within the Soviet Empire.[106] This was evidenced by the presence, in 1970, of an anarchist pirate radio station in Russia; the anarchist Left Opposition (LO) group in Leningrad between 1976 and 1978; and the Movement of Revolutionary Communards (MRC) that sprang up in the same city between 1979–1982 in the wake of the LO's suppression. In 1979, the Free General Workers' Union (SMOT), the first Russian syndicalist-influenced organisation to emerge in decades, was founded, and the MRC affiliated to it. Also in 1979, anarchists at the State University of Dnepropetrovsk in the Ukraine were arrested for attempting to establish a Communist League of Anarchists. Meanwhile, changes were afoot in other Soviet satellite regimes of Eastern Europe with the foundation of the clandestine Polish Anarchist Federation (FA) in 1988, and the Anarcho-Syndicalist Federation (ASF) in Czechoslovakia in 1989, just before the Marxist regime there collapsed. This was followed by the founding in 1991 of the Anarchist Federation (AF) which defiantly renamed itself the Czech and Slovak Anarchist Federation (CSAF) after the division of the country into the Czech Republic and Slovakia. Undoubtedly, there were anarcho- and revolutionary syndicalist influences on unions elsewhere in this time. For example, syndicalism was an influence, although not predominant, on the Federation of South African Trade Unions (FOSATU), founded in 1979.[107]

THE FONTENIST RESPONSE: THE "VANISHING VANGUARD" ADVANCES LIBERTARIAN COMMUNISM

The ideas of the *Platform*, which were expressed in essence again by the Friends of Durruti, have maintained the anarchist hard line time and again, especially when the movement has been in crisis. Following the defeat of the Spanish Revolution in 1939, many anarchist militants were disillusioned and a deathly anti-revolutionary liberalism that focused on "personal liberation," rather than class struggle, crept into the movement. In 1953, just after the anarchists had played a key role in initiating the Cuban Revolution, the French anarchist-communist militant George Fontenis wrote the *Manifeste du communisme libertaire* (*Manifesto of Libertarian Communism*) for the platformist Libertarian Communist Federation (FCL). The FCL's origins were clandestine, as the platformist tendency had arisen within the FAF in 1950, as a secret caucus called the Thought-Battle Organisation (OPB), of which Fontenis was the secretary. Fontenis later regretted this clandestinity, even though the synthesists had their own similar network within the FAF. The existence of the OPB only became known two years after it dramatically captured and overhauled the FAF at its 1952 Congress, transforming it into the FCL, with a minority of dissident synthesists leaving to reform the FAF the following year. The unaccountable secrecy of the OPB faction, which was apparently designed to attract the left flank of the French Communist Party, tarnished the debate over the *Manifesto*.

As with other platformist-style manifestos, the *Manifesto* caused an uproar, attacking the "synthesist" form of anarchist organising that included extreme individualism, alongside anarcho-syndicalism, and a mish-mash of libertarian ideas. It also rejected the usual Bolshevik theories of the dictatorship of the proletariat (actually the dictatorship of the party) and the two-stage revolution (actually the revolution put on hold forever). It affirmed anarchism as a class-struggle, revolutionary theory, and practice, and called for a disciplined "vanguard" to push the revolution forward. By vanguard, Fontenis did not mean the Marxist-styled, self-appointed "leaders" of the people, which he said "leads to a pessimistic evaluation of the role of the masses, to an aristocratic contempt for their political ability, to concealed direction of revolutionary activity, and so to defeat."

Instead, the *Manifesto*'s "vanguard" was defined as a revolutionary organisation tasked with "developing the direct political responsibility of the masses; it must aim to increase the masses' ability to organise themselves." As its final aim, this group of activists was "to disappear in becoming identical with the masses when they reach their highest level of consciousness in achieving the revolution." It would work within established mass organisations like unions, educational groups, mutual aid societies, and others, and actively propagate its ideas. Its basic principles would be ideological and tactical unity, collective action and discipline, and a federal, rather than centralised, structure.

In Italy, in the 1950s, hardline "organisational" anarchists founded the Proletarian Action Anarchist Groups (GAAP) within the synthesist Italian Anarchist Federation (FAI), and were later expelled. The GAAP did not survive for long on its own, but in its brief existence, the GAAP united with Fontenis' FCL and the North African Libertarian Movement (MLNA) of Morocco, Algeria, and Tunisia, to form a Libertarian Communist International (ICL) that was more of a Western Mediterranean organisation, and which collapsed with the simultaneous suppression of the FCL in France and the MLNA in Algeria in 1957. Despite the disappearance of a specific platformist tendency in Italy, veterans of the GAAP and the memory of its practice formed the backbone of today's Federation of Communist Anarchists (FdCA), founded in 1985.

Fontenis is a controversial character in France, but as an obituary states, he was "one of the leading figures in the postwar revolutionary movement in France. He played an important role in the reconstruction and reform of the French anarchist movement, and in supporting those fighting for Algerian independence in the 1950s and 60s; a prominent activist in May 68, he would go on to help (re)create a libertarian communist movement in the 1970s; he was also in later life one of the pillars of the *Libre Pensée* (*Free Thought*) movement; having joined the Union of Libertarian Communist Workers (UTCL) in 1980, he would subsequently become a member of *Alternative Libertaire*, and would remain a member until his death at the age of 90," in 2010. While platformism in France suffered from the suppression of the FCL in 1957—until its ideas were revived in 1968 with the founding of the Anarchist Revolutionary Organisation (ORA) tendency that split from the FAF in 1970—it remained a minority tendency within the Western anarchist movement. Its strong anti-imperialist credentials, which had been proven in the Algerian Liberation War, meant that it did find a powerful resonance within the Latin American anarchist movement, where it would again manage to establish mass organisations.

The ORA called itself "a federation of territorial or trades groups and not a gathering of individuals" and its *Organisational Contract* (1970) stated that "anarchism repudiates all authoritarianism: that of pure individualism with its repudiation of society, and that of pure communism which seeks to ignore the individual. Anarchism is not a synthesis of antagonistic principles, but a juxtaposition of concrete, living realities, the convergence of which must be sought in an equilibrium as elastic as life itself." While hailing the platformist principles of ideological and tactical unity, collective responsibility, rank-and-file decision-making, and libertarian federalism, the *Organisational Contract* stated that the ORA "has no pretensions to a rigid ideological unity generating dogmatism [or, what it named 'stodgy uniformity']. But on the other hand, it refuses also to be merely a motley collection of divergent tendencies, the frictions between which would inevitably lead to stagnation."

An *Addendum to the Organisational Contract* stated that the ORA "is to be the driving force behind mass movements against authoritarian systems" and it appears, in part, to have achieved this. The ORA inspired the creation of platformist organisations with the same acronym in Denmark in 1973 (since dissolved), Britain in the mid-1970s (since dissolved), and Italy in 1976, the last of which became the FdCA of today in 1985. The French ORA became today's French/Belgian Libertarian Communist Organisation (OCL) and its

Libertarian Alternative (AL) splinter. The longevity of the FdCA and ORA/OCL/AL lines help put paid to the idea that platformism is a disguised intermediary stage in a rightward capitulation towards Bolshevism.

In Latin America, as stated, platformism renewed its strength. Known as *especifismo* (specifism), in the southern cone of the continent, it developed the most powerful challenge to state-capitalist revolutionism, especially after the 1956 founding of the Uruguayan Anarchist Federation (FAU), which harkened back to an earlier federation of the same name, between the years 1938 and 1941. In 1972, the FAU produced the seminal text of *especifismo*, *Huerta Grande* (*Large Orchard*) which stressed the need to avoid "voluntarism" driven merely by good will, in favour of a political line informed by a sound analysis of the real conditions in Uruguay. In rejecting the creation of a new theory of action from scratch, *Huerta Grande* automatically rejected bourgeois and "fashionable" analyses out of hand, in favour of revolutionary socialist analyses that were directly applicable to the situation in Uruguay. Those analyses would then be linked to the ideological objectives of the FAU, in transforming Uruguayan society by its political praxis, although "only through it [praxis], through its concrete existence, in the tested conditions of its development, can we elaborate a useful theoretical framework."

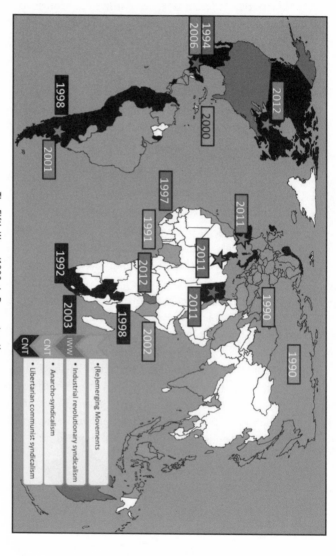

The Fifth Wave (1990–): Reconstruction

THE FIFTH WAVE, 1990–TODAY

THE ANARCHIST MOVEMENT'S RESURGENCE IN THE ERA OF SOVIET COLLAPSE AND NEOLIBERAL HEGEMONY

The Fourth Wave of anarchist insurgencies were crushed by neo-fascist repression in Latin America in the mid-1970s, as the US continued to fund death squads into the 1980s, and by the increasingly militarised response of many anarchists in Western Europe and North America, due to their isolation from the popular classes. This led many to embrace terrorism, Maoism, Third Worldism, and other deviations, but anarcho- and revolutionary syndicalism steadily rebuilt, as did anarchist political organisation. A Fifth Wave, far broader than the Fourth, was soon unleashed between 1989 and 1991, with the dramatic collapse of the Soviet Union and the liberation of its Eastern European satellite colonies, including the

Marxist oddity that was Albania and the Titoist dissident region of Yugoslavia. Immediately, the underground anarchist movement in those countries surged forth, with the Polish AF and the Czechoslovakian ASF, and with the Confederation of Anarcho-Syndicalists (KAS) and Confederation of Revolutionary Anarcho-Syndicalists (KRAS), both founded in Russia in 1989, leading the way. The explosion of new anarchist organisations in the former Soviet empire has been remarkable: from the Baltic states to the Balkan states, and Belarus to Kazakhstan, there is barely a region of the ex-USSR and its satellites which has not seen a newly emergent anarchist and anarcho-/revolutionary syndicalist movement. Notable is the establishment of organisations like the 2,000–strong Revolutionary Confederation of Anarcho-Syndicalists, Nestor Makhno (RKAS-NM) in former anarchist strongholds like the Ukraine, and the emergence of explicitly "Makhnovist" groups in countries like Greece and Turkey.

Geographically the broadest self-described "anarchist-communist" network in the world today, outside of the syndicalist union federations, is Autonomous Action (AD), with branches in 20 Russian cities, as well as in Armenia, Belarus, Kazakhstan, and Ukraine—although by my definition, AD is a synthesist organisation.[108] The ongoing development of underground anarcho-syndicalist networks under Marxist dictatorships, like that of Cuba, which are rapidly embracing liberal capitalism, demonstrates that we can expect a further emergence in times to come, especially as totalitarianism loses its grip in China, Vietnam, and North Korea. Although no current anarchist underground is known in those latter regions, in 1997, a Swedish SAC delegation to Cuba discovered there was an active indigenous anarcho-syndicalist underground. By the 2000s, the exile MLC was rebuilding itself and established the Aid Group for the Libertarians and Independent Syndicalists in Cuba (GALSIC), which, as Fidel Castro's health failed, began to publish the bulletin *Cuba Libertaria* (*Libertarian Cuba*) in 2004. The collapse of right-wing dictatorships in Latin America, left-wing dictatorships in Eastern Europe and Central Asia, the reactionary South Korean state, South African apartheid, and the emergence of militant new social movements, as capital contracts ever more severely into a neo-corporatist crisis, has spurred on the revival of *especifista* organisations in Argentina, Bolivia, Brazil, Colombia, Costa Rica, Chile, Ecuador, Mexico, Peru, Venezuela, and Uruguay, and the emergence of a platformist organisation in French Guiana. The primary organisation that helped initiate this spurt of new growth was the revived FAU of Uruguay, which rebuilt in 1985, repudiated its earlier pro-Castroism, and developed an *especifist* conception similar to the *Platform*. The result of its leading role in regenerating anarchist praxis in the southern cone of Latin America is that most of the region's most significant new organisations are *especifista/*platformist organisations.[109]

The Zapatista Revolt in Chiapas in southern Mexico in 1994, with its post-Soviet Makhnovist-like model of libertarian socialist, civilian, decentralised administration, defended by a militia, and its explicit references to the anarchist-influenced Zapatista Revolution of the 1910s, helped provide the impetus for the creation of neighbouring anarchist-indigenist organisations such as the Indigenous Popular Council of Oaxaca—Ricardo Flores Magón (CIPO-RFM) and its splinter

Magónista-Zapatista Alliance (AMZ). In Africa, the conditions of neo-colonialism lead to the construction of anarchist organisations, which often for the same reasons proved ephemeral; these include the Anarchist Party for Individual Freedoms in the Republic (PALIR) in Senegal in 1981, the fate of which is unknown to me, the Anarchist Workers' and Students' Group (ASWG) of Zambia in 1998 which did not survive the death of its founder, librarian Wilstar Choongo (1964–1999), and the *Wiyathi* Collective within the Anti-Capitalist Convergence of Kenya (ACCK) in the early 2000s. But the closing phases of resistance to militarism and apartheid saw the (re-)emergence of larger or more durable anarchist organisations where its heritage had been slender: the 3,240–strong IWW section among diamond miners in Sierra Leone in the early 1990s, which was sadly destroyed in 1997 by the civil war precipitated by a military coup d'état (the fate of members such as local delegate Bright Chikezi who were transported to Guinea by US Marines remaining unknown); the anarcho-syndicalist Awareness League (AL) of Nigeria, which rose to about 1,000 members in the oil and other industries during the General Sani Abacha dictatorship; and the Anarchist Resistance Movement (ARM), and Durban Anarchist Federation (DAF) of South Africa, the latter two being the forerunners of today's Zabalaza Anarchist Communist Front (ZACF), an *especifista* organisation founded in 2003 by myself and a multiracial group of anarchists, along Brazilian lines, which is still active today as a tiny, but prolific, ideologically influential core.[110]

Invigorated by the "Battle of Seattle" and public disgust at the US-led imperialist wars against Afghanistan and Iraq, the organised anarchist movement in North

America—long plagued by individualism, primitivism, and other anti-class-war ideologies—has rediscovered itself, notably with the founding of the North-Eastern Federation of Anarcho-Communists (NEFAC) of the USA/Canada in 2000, which sparked the creation of similar regional organisations across the continent. NE-FAC has since subdivided into three separate anarchist organisations, called the Common Struggle Libertarian Communist Federation in the US, Common Cause in Ontario, Canada, and the Libertarian Communist Union (UCL) in Québec, Canada.[111] The neoliberal crisis has seen the establishment of anarchist organisations in regions where there was no historical precedent or where the traditions were long-dead: from Lebanon to Sierra Leone, Costa Rica to Kenya, El Salvador to Zambia, Tunisia to the Dominican Republic, Jordan to Uganda.

A Fifth Wave of anarcho- and revolutionary syndicalism has arisen, despite the fractious debates that have cost the IWA its Japanese, Colombian, and factions of its French and Italian sections. This is apparent not only in the continued existence of the veteran anarcho-syndicalist organisations of Western Europe, such as the General Confederation of Labour (CGT) of Spain, which at 60,000 members is now the largest in the world (and the third-largest union federation in Spain, representing two million workers through workplace elections), the 6,000–strong Siberian Confederation of Labour (SKT), and the National Confederation of Labour—France (CNT-F), which claims 5,000 members. The Swedish Central Workers' Organisation (SAC) currently claims a membership of 9,000, a thousand fewer members than in the late 1990s, after it discontinued the practice of including members who had retired from their employment, but has embarked on an ambitious programme to re-invigourate the relevance of syndicalism in Sweden. In addition, there is the rank-and-file factory councilist/syndicalist tendency within a section of the union "base committee" movement of Italy (CIB-UNICOBAS), the alternative "struggle syndicalism" unions in France centred on the trade unions Solidarity Unity Democracy (SUD), and SUD in Switzerland which explicitly recognise revolutionary syndicalism as one of their main influences. Equally promising are the growing contacts being made between such formations, and a wide range of unions in Africa and Asia, ranging from the Democratic Republic of Congo to Malaysia, Burkina Faso to Bangladesh, which interact with the syndicalist movement.

New and old anarcho- and revolutionary syndicalist unions are collaborating continentally by sector (railways, communications, education etc.), across neoliberal "Fortress Europe," through the European Federation of Alternative Syndicalism—Education (FESAL-E) network of "grassroots syndicalist" teachers' unions.[112] This expansive Fifth Wave has seen numerous splinters, arguments, collapses, and reformations, but this is a sign of rapid growth and the development of a plethora of different libertarian, communist approaches to the challenges posed to the working class by turbo-capitalism in the new millennium.

Lastly, the current wave is also experiencing a period of intense international organising, with the formation of three new networks: International Libertarian Solidarity (ILS),[113] founded in 2001 (though defunct within the decade); the holding of a series of international anarcho-/revolutionary syndicalist conferences, in San Francisco in 1999, in Paris in 2000, in Essen in 2002, and in Paris in 2007—which have notably drawn in many emergent rank-and-file unions from West Africa; and perhaps of more significance from a Bakuninist dual-organisationist perspective, the establishment of the anarkismo.net news and analysis website in 2003.[114] The anarkismo project currently represents 33 "anarchist-communist," *especifista*, and platformist-inspired organisations from Argentina, Australia, Brazil, Canada, Colombia, Denmark, Ecuador, France/Belgium, Ireland, Italy, Norway, Mexico, Peru, South Africa, Switzerland, the United Kingdom, the United States of America, and Uruguay. The project's name is in the universalist Esperantist patois and its website publishes in French, Spanish, English, Portuguese, Turkish, German, Dutch, Norwegian, Arabic, Chinese, Russian, Polish and other languages, making it probably the most serious internationalist attempt to provide sound, multilingual anarchist analysis of social, economic, and political developments around the world today.

In countries such as France, where mass organisations were the rule, self-described platformist organisations have remained an important influence on the specific anarchist movement to the present day. In the 1970s, they spread across Europe, and, in the 1990s, to Latin America, the ex-Soviet empire, the Middle East, and Southern Africa. In the new millennium, the mainstream mass organisational tendency is again in ascendance. The lead given both by new organisations, such as Common Struggle and the Workers' Solidarity Movement (WSM) of Ireland, and older ones, such as the Uruguayan FAU and the Italian FdCA, have inspired a tremendous growth-spurt of anarchist-communist organising, marked by the Bakuninist/platformist/

especifista-influenced coherence of their critiques and practices. The new organisations have mushroomed, despite the revival by their antagonists of the hoary old claim that the tendency is crypto-Bolshevik.

There is no real platformist international because, as I have shown, platformism is primarily an organisational tactic within anarchism, dating back to the Bakuninist stress on dual organisationism, rather than an ideological orientation in its own right. But the aforementioned organisations—networked together loosely as the international editorial collective of the anarkismo project—work alongside the unaligned (and where possible, the IWA-aligned) anarcho-syndicalist and specific anarchist organisations. It is also worth noting the rise of specific anarchist political organisations in parts of the world where the anarchist tradition is more slender historically or did not previously exist: Costa Rica, Estonia, French Guyana, Israel/Palestine, Lebanon, Iran and the Iranian Diaspora, Turkey, Slovakia, Swaziland (ZACF), and Zimbabwe. Also, the "Arab Spring" has resulted in the emergence of at least one new anarchist specific organisation in the Arab world: the Libertarian Socialist Movement (LSM) in Egypt.[115]

THE *ESPECIFISTA* RESPONSE: THE ANARCHIST "ENGINE" THAT DRIVES PEOPLE'S POWER TOWARDS REVOLUTIONARY RUPTURE

In 1991, following the collapse of Soviet state capitalism, the French platformist Libertarian Alternative (AL) took up the pro-organisational torch with *Manifeste pour une Alternative Libertaire* (*Manifesto for a Libertarian Alternative*).[116] Its aim was not only to help inject a hardline perspective into the growing anarchist movement, but to show other true revolutionaries a way out of the dead end into which state "socialism" had led the workers. It dealt with the issues faced by the modern working class under neoliberalism: mass unemployment, casualisation, neo-colonialism, the enclosure of the people's "commons" down to the genetic level, the rise of the new technical middle class (computer specialists, etc.), and so forth. It emphasised the need for a worker-driven revolutionary project that would aim to dismantle capitalism and all forms of oppression, including those directed against women. Like the *Platform*, it also called for "statutory rules," in order that the anarchist organisation might run efficiently and co-ordinate its external activities. These rules would be based on "a common identity" and strategies would be worked out by free discussion among all members.

In 1993, five years after the fall of the Berlin Wall, the FAU, which had rebuilt itself a decade previously after the collapse of the dictatorship, adopted the *Declaración de Principios de FAU* (*Declaration of Principles of the FAU*) at its 10th Congress in Montevideo. The *Declaration* of the Congress opened by stating, "The vision of anarchism advocated by the FAU is built around a critique of relations of domination in all spheres of social activity (political, economic, legal, military, educational, cultural, etc.)." Despite capitalism lurching from one crisis to the next, the *Declaration* stated, anarchism had proven its resilience, so against a fatalistic doctrine of the inevitability of capitalist collapse, the anarchists posed a doctrine of human agency, the "meaning of will, of action, of the individual and collective consciousness of the oppressed." The end of the Soviet Empire and the rise of American hegemony—"the Cold War served both the US and the USSR to reassert its hegemony in their respective areas of influence, and internally, to perpetuate a system of privilege and coercion"—had ushered in an era of volatile financial capital destabilising entire regions, driving "chronic hunger and social catastrophes expressed in local wars"—the statist/capitalist responses to which the writers of the *Declaration* referred included

> a strengthening and automation of instruments of repression and control are now moving towards what they call 'low intensity conflicts', a kind of preventive repression to prevent the outbreak and spread of conflicts, usually desperate corollaries of social situations. Simultaneously, in other areas is the strengthening of authoritarian forms in response to social instability. Similarly, diffuse conceptions of society conceived as a vertical structure, ultra-hierarchical and static. This is the case of some ideological responses that are based on religious beliefs. Perhaps less tangible, but equally widespread is the crisis afflicting the world in virtually all political parties, caste politics and the instruments of political mediation. It is partly this crisis that has fuelled the resurgence of authoritarian populist movements… This feeling, perversely fed clearly fascist-inspired groups and movements. Again flourish anti-Semitism, xenophobia and racism, and the uncertainty of tomorrow takes refuge in an ultra aggressive nationalism.

The depth and range of the discussion of interpenetrated issues in the *Declaration* demonstrates the maturity reached by the FAU—well beyond the simplicity of the *Huerta Grande*—after being forged in the fires of repression that murdered so many of its members. For the purpose of this essay, I will only focus, however, on their view of their own role. The *Declaration* states:

> The FAU is intended as a political expression of the class interests of the dominated, exploited and oppressed, and is located at their service and aspires to be an engine of social struggles, an engine that neither represents nor replaces [in other words, does not substitute itself for the class]... For us, the political organisation is also the area where the experience of popular struggle accumulates, both domestically and internationally, an instance that prevents the dilution of the knowledge that the exploited and oppressed acquire over time.

In other words, the specific organisation is the repository of the oppressed classes' experience of struggle, struggle that in and of itself constitutes the revolutionary gymnasium wherein the class tests its strength for the overturning of the capitalist world order. The *Declaration* averred that "The political organisation... is well placed to take on the different and complex levels of activity that may require revolutionary work, the only body able to ensure all technical, material, political, theoretical, and so on requirements which are *sine qua non* of a strategy of rupture." The rupture spoken of here lies at the heart of *especifismo*. The specific organisation's primary task is to sever the ideological, political, social, and economic bonds that bind the oppressed classes to the parasitic classes, and this rupture constitutes the counter-cultural breach between the opposed forces, creating

the foundation on which revolutionary decentralist anarchist-communist counter-power can be built.

The *Declaration* continues:

> Our vision of the political organisation is contrary
> to the various forms of "modernism" of "depositors
> of consciousness" in short, self-appointed groups
> who feel touched by the finger of god. The organi-
> sation, maintaining and promoting the spirit of re-
> volt, endorsing all the present and future demands
> of a revolutionary process, hails from militant or-
> ganised labour and can only promote consistently
> and with redoubled force the creation, strengthen-
> ing and consolidation of grassroots organisations,
> which form the core of a people's power revolu-
> tion… And finally, in the strict domain of political
> action… the FAU aspires to be the tool for realising
> our libertarian principles.

Going on to speak of "the organisation as a school
of life," "of ethics, in accordance with the values we es-
pouse," the *Declaration* states that the "FAU is not a fin-
ished organisation, it is rather a project. In this sense,
it is also a life-plan that attracts the men and women
of our people willing to find ways of a better and more
humane existence [it is] a constant forge, which is not
decreed once and for all, bur that is produced in a constant revolutionary effort."

In 2005, the Italian militant schoolteacher Saverio
Crapraro, member of the FdCA, produced *Comunisti
Anarchici: Una Questione di Classe (Anarchist-Communists: A Question of Class)*,[117] which spelled out the
key theoretical bases of the idea, tracing a lineage from

Bakunin to Luigi Fabbri to Camillo Berneri. Luigi Fabbri (1877–1935), a prolific anarchist writer and long-time associate of Malatesta died during the Fascist era in exile in Uruguay where his daughter the anarchist writer and publisher Luce Fabbri (1908–2000) was involved with the synthesist ALU splinter off the FAU. Camillo Berneri (1897–1937), an anarchist philosopher, theorist and activist—held by many Italian anarchists to be Malatesta's ideological heir—fought in the resistance to the Fascists until 1926 when he fled Italy. He was murdered by the Bolsheviks during the Spanish Revolution. Crapraro's *A Question of Class* tied this rather Italianate lineage to the experiments of the Paris Commune, and the Ukrainian and Spanish Revolutions. It argued for distinctions between not only Bakuninism and the Left, but between it and other "anarchist" tendencies, using a method of historical materialism. *A Question of Class* argued for organisational dualism of the specific organisation working within the mass organisation, stating that

> The relationship between the masses and their most conscious elements (the vanguard) is one of the fundamental problems regarding the formulation of a revolutionary strategy. The absence of a solution to this problem, or incorrect solutions to it, lie behind every historical failure of each revolutionary project or else are the basis of the failures in those countries where revolutions enjoyed some initial success. No school of Marxism has yet clarified that relationship in its essence, and while on the part of Anarchists, the rejection a priori of the concept of a vanguard (a word which evokes an unwarranted idea of authority) has long impeded any detailed explanation.

The only clear thinking on the matter remains, even after over a century, Bakunin.

The FdCA position paper goes on to state that:

The capitalist system has perfected a series of in-struments with which it can recover what it loses to workers' demands, so it is perfectly utopian to claim that the material needs [of the proletariat] and their satisfaction can automatically provoke the end of capitalism, ruined by its internal contradictions. The struggle for material needs must also be the seed for class consciousness and the basis on which a de-tailed strategy for attacking the capitalist system can be grounded. It must also be a revolutionary strate-gy, which can be a point of reference for the political growth of the proletariat in the struggle and ensure an increase in those struggles as part of a strategic process which will direct them towards the goal of the revolution. An organisation is therefore required for the development of strategy and this organisa-tion (the specific organisation) of revolutionary pro-letarians must be based on a common theory. This is organisational dualism.

Crapraro goes on to say that the defining features of the mass organisation, that which "the masses build for their defence of their interests are: heterogeneity, due to the fact that its goal, independently of the political ideas of its members, is not to unite people who are already members of this party or that but to unite all workers who share the interests to be defended; [and] direct ac-tion, by which we mean the first-hand running of the struggles and agreement on demands, as a constant practice, in other words by the workers. The labour union, as a mass organisation, is therefore a tool in the hands of the working classes for the improvement of their economic conditions and for their emancipation, through anti-capitalist struggle." It is neither the creation nor toy of the specific organisation, or the exclusive preserve of revolutionaries, but an all-embracing organisation of class. He goes on to describe the tasks of the specific organisation "to be the depository for the class memory" and "to elaborate a common strategy which can ensure the linking of all the struggles and which can stimulate and guide." But the specific organisation, for Crapraro and the FdCA, is neither a Leninist party which sits above the masses, nor a mere connector of struggles, lacking a strategy of its own; rather the organisation is a "party-guide" that "establishes a political line which is then transmitted to the [mass] organisations, like a drive belt."

Dockworkers in Buenos Aires during the 1919 Revolt in Argentina

Autre Futur anarchist & syndicalist congress in Paris, 2000

CONCLUSION

THE ROLE OF THE ANARCHIST SPECIFIC ORGANISATION IN A "FRONT OF OPPRESSED CLASSES"

By involvement in everyday struggles, we build tomorrow today, a new world in the shell of the old, and create a dual-power situation as exists now in Argentina: popular power of the base undermines the parasitic power of the bourgeoisie. History is not neutral. In school, we are told that we need governments and bosses. We are told that history is a struggle between different governments, armies, and ruling elites. We are told that only the rich and powerful make history. What we are not told is that ordinary people have fought the bosses and rulers every step of the way and that this class war is the true engine of civilisation and progress. We are not

told that governments and capitalism are not only unnecessary, but destructive of all that is worthwhile. We,
as anarchists, know that people, even the bourgeoisie,
are not inherently bad; we all merely conform to our
class interests. Given the right conditions, conditions of
true equality and freedom, a powerful spirit of mutual
aid and co-operation has been demonstrated to come to
the fore in the popular masses.

How we act is related to the structure of society. When
oppression and exploitation are forcibly removed by directly-democratic, horizontally-federated organisations
operating under the guidance of the popular will, then
the "goodness" that is in most of us comes through and
flourishes as it did when the workers held the reigns in
Argentina, Macedonia, Ukraine, Spain, Mexico, Manchuria, China, Iran, Cuba, France, Nicaragua, Bolivia,
Algeria, and elsewhere. I hope that I have shown that
what we anarchists are putting forward are not just pretty,
unrealistic ideas. I hope I have indicated with this brief introduction to the broad anarchist movement's rich history
that these ideas can work; a new society can be created
with the workers, peasants, and the poor in control.

But it won't happen spontaneously—we must organise for it. That is why we need revolutionary organisations that draw together all those fighting for workers'
control of the means of production and directly-democratic community self-organisation, organisations that
give us the chance to exchange ideas and experiences
and to learn from the lessons of history. We do not need
groups of pushy leaders and their passive followers. As
Rosa Luxemburg said in *Organisational Questions of the
Russian Social Democracy*: "Let us put it quite bluntly:
the errors committed by a truly revolutionary workers'

movement are historically far more fruitful and valuable than the infallibility of even the best central committee."[118] We do not need elite political caucuses and "vanguard parties" dictating to us from on high. What we need are working class organisations under workers' directly-democratic control, with strictly-mandated delegates, subject to rank-and-file decision-making, mobilising the mass of ordinary people, in the process of making a truly social, grassroots revolution, with communes/soviets and syndicalist unions federated horizontally across urban and rural areas, defended by an armed militia, under the pluralistic civilian control of mass organisations of the class. These, in turn, are invigorated by specific organisations of anarchist tendency, on the grounds laid out by Bakunin and his followers, along the lines of platformism/*especificismo*.

A most important point is, however, that anarchists are not, and should not, be the sole organisers of the working class in preparation for revolution. To put it plainly, we anarchists are not fighting for an anarchist world, but a free world, and we are not the only social force moving in a libertarian direction. We need to be deeply and intimately involved in the global, anti-neoliberal movement and in the practical day-to-day struggles of the working class, demonstrating mutual aid, solidarity, responsibility, federalism, and all the other principles of revolutionary anarchism in action.

This point was made by the anarchist group Rebel Libertarian Socialism (*Auca*-SL) of Argentina, in its *Declaration of Principles* (1998): "the model of the Single Revolutionary Party is exhausted. It has demonstrated its lack of flexibility against the different political manifestations of our class." In opposition to this traditional, narrow-minded political idea of the role of the revolutionary organisation, *Auca*-SL promoted the idea of a "Front of Oppressed Classes [FOC] where syndicalist, social and political models which, in general, struggle for revolutionary change will converge. It is there, in the heart of the FOC, where a healthy debate of political tendencies and positions should be engaged in, so that the course the FOC takes is representative of the existing correlation of popular forces." The FOC idea is totally different from the Popular Front idea, common to Marxist-Leninists, in which they form a front organisation supposedly for solidarity purposes, then insert their leaders to rule this commandeered social force, which they then order about like an army. Instead, the anarchist FOC concept represents the progressive, political plurality, anti-authoritarian solidarity, and innovative diversity of a united working class, in action against both capital and its Siamese twin, the state. *Auca*-SL warned against any bureaucratisation of the social struggle along Marxist-Leninist lines.

The FdCA's *A Question of Class* echoes this point, defining the specific organisation as "An organisation which is an internal part of the mass organisation and not external to it means that members of the specific organisation must be class-struggle militants. It does not substitute the masses in revolutionary action, but rather stimulates their political growth, their desire for self-management and self-organisation, leading to a revolutionary project. It is an inspiring, energetic force within the mass organisation to which it brings its strategy. For the very reason that members of the specific organisation are also members of the mass organisation, as members of the mass organisation, they bring to it their points of view in order that the action of the masses can be strategically co-ordinated, with the aim of reaching the revolutionary objective in the most efficient way possible."

Importantly, *A Question of Class* states: "[w]e defend other progressive organisations that are involved in struggles from repression. Where necessary, we will engage in United Front [similar to the FOC concept] actions alongside them." However, whilst we anarchists should defend these groups unconditionally, we should not do so uncritically—we must maintain our independence and argue for Bakuninist ideas. The natural skills, intelligence, innovation, and solidarity owned by the working class are the only things that can produce both the social revolutionary dynamite needed to destroy the neo-corporatist neoliberal system—and the fertiliser that will enrich the post-revolutionary soil, so that it comes up roses: beautiful, but armed with thorns. The renewed energy, potency, and practicality of the anarchist movement has seen new organisations spreading like wildfire. As with the New Left of the Fourth Wave, this is taking place so much more deliberately and clearly today, through the contemporary Fifth Wave global anti-capitalist movement.

The working class is re-opening the anarchist/syndicalist toolbox of federated direct democracy, filled with tools carefully polished and maintained over the decades by a dedicated militant minority, to rediscover not only the most effective forms of directly-democratic resistance, but the cultural forms that sustained a decentralised form of popular power. Now that millions of people are excluded from the globally uniform, pay-to-enjoy spectacle of capitalist culture, many are turning to self-generated counter-culture, in all its locally-specific diversity, to sustain their new vision of a self-empowered, counter-power world. The realisability of this vision has become tangible again, and so its message more commanding of attention. In 1848, Karl Marx and Friedrich Engels' *Manifesto of the Communist Party* argued that a "new spectre," the "spectre of communism," was "haunting" Europe. Today, to judge from the mainstream press, a "new spectre," that of revolutionary anarchism, haunts the halls of power across the world of neoliberal capitalism—showing its vaunted hegemony to be a lie. As an issue of the *New York Times* a decade ago had it, anarchism remains "the idea that would not die."

ACKNOWLEDGMENTS

I have been greatly aided in writing this essay—a brief overview of the broad anarchist movement's primary challenges and organisational responses over the past 15 decades—by excellent and groundbreaking work done by specialists in a wide range of fields, especially new sociological and transnational labour studies. In particular, I need to thank Lucien van der Walt, my co-author on the *Counter-power* books, my editor Marie-Eve Lamy and translator Alexandre Sánchez of Lux Éditeur in Montreal who prepared the first, French, edition, as well as my editor Stef Gude, and Kate Khatib of AK Press who prepared this edition, for their rigorous and useful comments which substantially improved my text. In my research into the movement's historical record,

I have also been greatly assisted by the opening of the Russian state archives, which, while reportedly in a rather chaotic condition, have allowed penetrating new analyses to be compiled by historians searching for the truth behind 70 years of Soviet myth-making; much of this exciting new research originates in Canada and France. In addition, I am greatly indebted to the invaluable contribution of anarchist veterans themselves, particularly those who fought against dictatorship in Bulgaria in the 1940s (Jack Grancharoff), in Spain in the 1960s and 1970s (Octavio Alberola Suriñach and Stuart Christie), in Uruguay (Juan Carlos Mechoso and Ruben Tastas Duque), in Chile and in Argentina in the 1970s, and in Iran (Payman Piedar) and Iraq (SB) in the same period, for filling in gaps that countless militants died to bridge—but also to the rising stars of contemporary anarchist and revolutionary syndicalist militancy, both those who are acknowledged theorists, and those rank-and-file operators who never see the limelight. And lastly, I have drawn extensively on standard and more obscure movement literature and histories, many of them detailed here in the footnotes, while recognising their limitations as partisan documents.

NOTES

1   The First International, the informal name of the International Workingmen's Association (IWMA) of 1864–1877, was the first significant international socialist organisation to unite trade unions and militants across national lines. It split in 1872 into an anarchist majority organisation and a Marxist minority faction.

2   Nancy Fraser, *Rethinking the Public Sphere: A Contribution to the Critique of Actually Existing Democracy*, Duke University Press, Durham, USA, 1990; her ideas are updated in Nancy Fraser, *Transnationalizing the Public Sphere: On the Legitimacy and Efficacy of Public Opinion in a Post-Westphalian World*, 2007, online at http://eipcp.net/transversal/0605/fraser/en.

3   Buenaventura Durruti (1896–1936), interviewed by Pierre van Passen of the *Toronto Star* on 5 August 1936.

4   Steven Hirsch, *Anarcho-Syndicalist Roots of a Multi-Class Alliance: Organized Labor and the Peruvian Aprista Party 1900–1933*, PhD thesis, George Washington University Press, Washington DC, USA, 1997.

5   On the theory of anarchism as some sort of timeless primordial spirit of revolt, see Peter Marshall, *Demanding the Impossible: A History of Anarchism*, HarperCollins, London, UK, 2008. While a very valuable reference, Marshall's book uses a broader and more vague definition of anarchism than I do, drawing in many tendencies that, while they may be libertarian, antedate the formation of the First International, are often only linked by their common anti-statism, and are totally incompatible on innumerable other issues.

6   This quote is from his essay *Statism and Anarchy*, 1873, quoted in Sam Dolgoff (ed), *Bakunin on Anarchy*, George Allen and Unwin, London, UK, 1971. The best new study is Mark Leier, *Bakunin: The Creative Urge; A Biography*, Publishers Group Canada, Toronto, 2006. Bakunin's ideas on anarchist organisation can be found specifically in the *Rules and Programme of the International Alliance of Socialist Democracy* (1868), and the *Programme of the International Brotherhood* (1869), both available online at http://anarchistplatform.wordpress.com.

7   Bakunin, quoted in Dolgoff, *Bakunin on Anarchy*.

8   For a groundbreaking series of case studies of anarchist engagements on the national question in Africa, Asia, colonial Europe (Ireland and Ukraine), and Latin America, read Lucien van der Walt and Steven J. Hirsch (eds), *Anarchism and Syndicalism in the Colonial and Postcolonial World: The Praxis of National Liberation, Internationalism and Social Revolution*, Brill, The Netherlands, 2010. A similarly broad series of case studies is due to be published shortly on the roots and adaptations of anarchism across the globe, José Antonio Guttiérez Dantón (ed), *Las Vertiente de la Anarquía*, Libros de Anarres, Buenos

Aires, Argentina, (due in 2013).

9   Giuseppe Fanelli (1827–1877), an Italian anarchist agita-
    tor and member of Bakunin's International Brotherhood
    who had fought with Garibaldi's forces, and in the Polish
    Revolt of 1862–1863.

10 Harmut Rübner, *Occupational Culture, Conflict Patterns
    and Organizational Behaviour: Perspectives of Syndicalism
    in 20ᵗʰ Century Shipping*, revised version of paper present-
    ed at "Syndicalism: Swedish and Historical Experiences,"
    Department of Economic History, Stockholm Universi-
    ty, 13–14 March 1998.

11 F. N. Brill, in *A Brief History of the IWW outside the US
    1905–1999*, IWW, USA, 1999, online at www.iww.org/
    en/history/library/misc/FNBrill1999, cites IWW activities
    in sites such as Chile, China, Cuba, Ecuador, Fiji, Ger-
    many, Japan, Peru, Siberia, and Sierra Leone. Brill's list is
    far from exhaustive: for a study of seaboard syndicalism in
    Cape Town, South Africa, read Lucien van der Walt, *Anar-
    chism and Syndicalism in an African Port City: the Revolu-
    tionary Traditions of Cape Town's Multiracial Working Class,
    1904–1931*, Labour History, Routledge, UK, 2011.

12 Bert Altena, *Analysing Revolutionary Syndicalism: the
    Importance of Community*, conference paper, Anarchist
    Studies Network, UK, 1999, since updated in *New Per-
    spectives on Anarchism, Labour and Syndicalism*, David
    Berry and Constance Bantam (eds), Cambridge Scholars
    Publishing, Newcastle-on-Tyne, UK, 2010.

13 The Haymarket Martyrs were seven Central Labor Union
    anarchist militants framed and executed by the US state
    in 1887 (an eighth committed suicide in jail). The in-
    ternational workers' festival of May Day commemorates
    their murders.

14 The CGT's *Charter of Amiens*, a famous position state-
    ment of revolutionary syndicalism, helped spark the Sec-
    ond Wave explosion of anarcho-syndicalism across Latin
    America, but had the notable weakness of being hostile

to politicking in the trade unions—even by anarchists—creating an "apolitical syndicalism" vulnerable to capture by reformists.

15   The uprising of the Kronstadt Soviet at the naval base near St. Petersburg in 1921 is widely seen as the last-ditch attempt to reinvigourate the proletarian Russian Revolution against the dictatorship of the Bolsheviks. Its key position statement in favour of pluralistic direct democracy exercised by free soviets, the *Petropavlovsk Resolution* taken by the 1st & 2nd Squadrons of the Baltic Fleet, is available in Daniel Guérin (ed), *No Gods No Masters: An Anthology of Anarchism, Book 2*, AK Press, Oakland, USA, 1998.

16   The Spanish Revolution is usually misrepresented in the literature as the *only* historical example of the anarchist movement exercising control over large tracts of territory (in particular, the cantons of Catalonia, Aragon, and Andalucia), but as I shall demonstrate in this essay, the thesis of "Spanish exceptionalism" is belied by the mass anarchist territorial control achieved in parts of Mexico, Manchuria, and the Ukraine in particular. Also, the capitulation of the Spanish mass movement to the machinations of their statist Republican allies, a huge strategic error that led directly to the defeat of the Revolution, remains insufficiently interrogated by anarchists themselves. Still, the Spanish situation remains the best-studied example of the pragmatic anarchist "administration of things" in running large industrial cities such as Barcelona, in the implantation of communal land-ownership in Aragon, and in the directly-democratic practices of its frontline militia.

17   The 1968 Revolt was far from limited to France: in many respects it was a global uprising that marked the definitive entrance onto the stage of history of youth as a distinct political force.

18   The most powerful East European movements were the

Bulgarian and the Polish—more on these later—but the other movements in the region (and in Scandinavia) were minority tendencies at best, although they fought an honourable battle against authoritarian regimes in Finland and the Baltic states, Yugoslavia, Greece and the Balkan states, Austria, Hungary, and Czechoslovakia. For example, the Swedish Central Workers' Organisation (SAC), founded in 1910 and still active today, peaked at only 32,000 members in 1920, while the anarcho-syndicalist faction within the General Workers' Confederation of Greece (GSEE) represented one in eight members in 1918.

19 On Egypt, read Anthony Gorman, "'Diverse in race, religion and nationality... but united in aspirations of civil progress': the anarchist movement in Egypt 1860–1940," and on South Africa, read Lucien van der Walt, "Revolutionary syndicalism, communism and the national question in South African socialism, 1886–1928," both available in Hirsch and van der Walt, 2010. And for a comparative analysis between North Africa and Southern Africa, but which covers other parts of the continent too, read Michael Schmidt and Lucien van der Walt, "Roots and Adaptations of Anarchism and Syndicalism in Africa 1870—the Present," in Gutiérrez Dantón (ed), due in 2012.

20 On the transnational linkages between Central America and the Caribbean, read Kirk Shaffer, "Tropical Libertarians: anarchist movements and networks in the Caribbean, Southern United States, and Mexico, 1890s-1920," in Hirsch and Van der Walt, 2010.

21 On Australia and New Zealand, read Verity Burgman, *Revolutionary Industrial Unionism: the Industrial Workers of the World in Australia*, Cambridge University Press, Cambridge, UK, 1995; and Erik Olsen, *The Red Feds: Revolutionary Industrial Unionism and the New Zealand Federation of Labour 1908–14*, Oxford University Press, Auckland, New Zealand, 1988; and Francis Schor, "Left Labor Agitators in the Pacific Rim of the Early Twentieth

Century," *International Labor and Working Class History*, No. 67, USA, Spring 2005.

22   On Vietnam, the most important work is Hue-Tam Ho Tai, *Radicalism and the Origins of the Vietnamese Revolution*, Harvard University Press, Cambridge, Massachusetts, USA, and London, UK, 1992. On the Philippines and its environs, read Benedict Anderson, *Under Three Flags: Anarchism and the Anti-colonial Imagination*, Verso, London, UK, and New York, USA, 2005. On Malaysia, read C.F. Yong, "Origins and Development of the Malaysian Communist Movement 1919–1930," *Modern Asian Studies*, Vol.5, No.4, Cambridge University Press, Cambridge, UK, October 1991.

23   On South Asia, specifically Hindustan in India, read Maia Ramnath, *Haj to Utopia: How the Ghadar Movement Charted Global Radicalism and Attempted to Overthrow the British Empire*, California World History Library, USA, 2011; and Maia Ramnath, *Decolonizing Anarchism: an Antiauthoritarian History of India's Liberation Struggle*, AK Press and Institute for Anarchist Studies, USA, 2011.

24   On the Levant, specifically Lebanon/Syria and Egypt, read the groundbreaking work of Ilham Khuri-Makdisi, *Levantine Trajectories: the Formulation and Dissemination of Radical Ideas in and between Beirut, Cairo and Alexandria 1860–1914*, Harvard University, 2003.

25   Lucien van der Walt and Michael Schmidt, *Black Flame: the Revolutionary Class Politics of Anarchism and Syndicalism*, AK Press, Oakland, USA, 2009. The book's blog is at http://black-flame-anarchism.blogspot.com.

26   Michael Schmidt and Lucien van der Walt, *Global Fire: 150 Fighting Years of International Anarchism and Syndicalism*, AK Press, Oakland, USA (forthcoming).

27   The best online archive of materials by and about Makhno and the Makhnovists is at www.nestormakhno.info. A selection of Makhno's writings is to be found in Alexandre

Skirda (ed) and Paul Sharkey (trans), *The Struggle Against the State and Other Essays*, 1996, online at www.ditext.com/makhno/struggle/struggle.html.

28   On the emergence of a distinctly anarchist mass movement within the First International read the Robert Graham chapter in Gutiérrez Dantón (ed), due in 2013. On the claiming of either Proudhon or Bakunin as the progenitor of the anarchist movement, read the David Berry chapter in Gutiérrez Dantón (ed)—and compare it to the arguments in Van der Walt and Schmidt, 2009.

29   On the birth of the organised anarchist movement in Spain, rooted in traditions of communalism and associationism, read the Luis Baños chapter in Gutiérrez Dantón (ed), due in 2013, and on the First Wave Spanish anarchist movement, read M. Molnár and J. Pekmez, *Rural Anarchism in Spain and the 1873 Cantonalist Revolution,* in Henry A Landsburger (ed), *Rural Protest: Peasant Movements and Social Change,* International Institute for Labour Studies, Macmillan, London, UK, 1974.

30   On the First and Second Wave Mexican anarchist movement, the premiere text is John M. Hart, *Anarchism and the Mexican Working Class 1860–1931,* University of Texas Press, Austin, USA, 1978, but a good overview is provided in the early chapters of Norman Caulfield, *Mexican Workers and the State: From the Porfiriato to NAFTA,* Texas Christian University Press, USA, 1998.

31   On the First Wave Uruguayan anarchist movement, Marshall writes: "As early as 1875 the Regional Federation of the Eastern Republic of Uruguay affiliated with the Bakuninist anti-authoritarian International which emerged from the split at the Hague Conference. From this time anarchism in Uruguay held sway in the workers' movement and revolutionary circles until the end of the 1920s."

32   On the First Wave Cuban anarchist movement, read Joan Casanovas Codina, *Labor & Colonialism in Cuba,* doctoral dissertation, State University of New York, USA,

1994; Gerald E Poyo, "The Anarchist Challenge to the Cuban Independence Movement 1885–1890," *Cuban Studies*, 15:1, Winter 1985; and Frank Fernández, *Cuban Anarchism: The History of Movement*, See Sharp Press, USA, 2001, online at http://libcom.org/library/cuba-anarchism-history-of-movement-fernandez.

33   On the roots and distinct influence of the American movement, read Kevin Saliger in Gutiérrez Dantón (ed), due in 2013, while on the First, Second and Third Wave American anarchist movement, read Kenyon Zimmer, *The Whole World Is Our Country: Immigration and Anarchism in the United States, 1885–1940*, University of Pittsburgh, USA, 2005.

34   Daniel De Leon (1852–1914), a Socialist Labor Party (SLP) leader and union organiser whose version of revolutionary syndicalism combined industrial unionist direct action with a socialist party electoral take-over of political power. Splitting from the IWW in 1908 over its rejection of political action, he formed what was nicknamed the "Detroit IWW," opposed to the majority "Chicago IWW," and the schism was replicated in other parts of the IWW world. Although as a person, De Leon himself was a staunch Marxist, in practice the Detroit IWW was sufficiently revolutionary syndicalist to fall within van der Walt and my definition of the "broad anarchist tradition."

35   David Footman, *Red Prelude—A Biography of Zhelyabov*, Barrie & Rockcliff, The Cresset Press, London, 1968, first published 1944. The NWU was founded by the joiner Stepan Khalturin (1857–1882). The son of a peasant, he became involved in subversive activities three years before founding the union, which was, according to Footman, "the first serious attempt in Russia to form a trade union. [Khalturin] was a man of intelligence and energy and secured some sixty members and a number of sympathisers." Footman asserts that it had a notable influence on the attitude of the *Narodnaya Volya* to organised labour, with *narodnik* leader Andrei Zhelyabov declaring that "in

Russia, a strike is a political act." Khalturin was opposed to terrorism, and the NWU purchased its own press, but before it could start printing, it was betrayed by a double-agent and a police raid shut the NWU and its press down in 1879, arresting all but Khalturin who later became a *Narodnaya Volya* militant and was executed as such in 1882. On the transitional politics of these early Russian initiatives during the First Wave, read the Frank Mintz chapter in Gutiérrez Dantón (ed), due in 2013.

36 The *narodniks* were social revolutionaries whose praxis was to immerse themselves in the peasantry and to fight the state by terrorism. The movement, which had many women members including the anarchist and later Marxist Vera Zasulich (1852–1919), gave birth to Russian anarchism, nihilism, and Marxism, a process detailed in Footman, 1968.

37 Followers of Louis Auguste Blanqui (1805–1881), a French revolutionary whose vision involved a small group of conspirators seizing power by coup d'etat rather than through the action of the masses, a strategy ridiculed by Marx but approximated in many respects by V.I. Lenin's Bolsheviks.

38 On the Cantonalist Revolt, read Molnár and Pekmez, 1974.

39 The standard biography of Kropotkin remains Martin A. Miller, *Kropotkin*, University of Chicago Press, Chicago, USA, 1976.

40 On the Haymarket affair, read Paul Avrich, *The Haymarket Tragedy*, Princeton University Press, Princeton, USA, 1986; and anonymous, *The Anarchists of Chicago: Haymarket 1886–1986*, Freedom centennial pamphlet, London, UK, 1986. For the radicalising influence of the hangings on generations of the American labour movement, read the Kevin Saliger chapter in Gutiérrez Dantón (ed), due in 2013.

41 The *Programme and Object of the Secret Revolutionary Organisation of the International Brotherhood*, is available online

at http://anarchistplatform.wordpress.com/2010/06/17/
the-program-of-the-international-brotherhood.

42 'International Revolutionary Society or Brotherhood," in
Daniel Guérin (ed), *No Gods, No Masters, Book One*, AK
Press, Oakland, USA,1998.

43 In 1910, the Belgian colonial authorities established a
Bourse du Travail in the eastern Zairean mining province
of Katanga in order to try and control the labour force
there, but it is suggested in Aldwin Roes, *The Bourse du
Travail de Katanga: A Parastatal Recruitment Organisation
with Monopolistic Powers? State-capital relations in the Mo-
bilisation of Katanga's Labour Power. 1910–1914*, London
School of Economics, 2007, that this stratagem in fact
enabled Kantangan labour to organise itself against the
employers—indicating possible syndicalist influence.

44 For a sound explanation of the tragic trajectory of the
Second Wave CGT from revolutionary syndicalism to
reformism, read Wayne Thorpe, "Uneasy Family: Revolutionary Syndicalism in Europe from the Charte de
Amiens to World War I," in in *New Perspectives on Anarchism, Labour and Syndicalism: the Individual, the National and the Transnational,* Berry and Bantman (eds),
Newcastle upon Tyne, UK, 2010, online at: http://
www.c-s-p.org/flyers/978-1-4438-2393-7-sample.pdf.
Picking up the story from there into the Third Wave is
David Berry, *A History of the French Anarchist Movement,
1917–1945,* AK Press, Oakland, USA, 2009.

45 The standard anarchist history of the Macedonian Revolt
is Georges Balkansky, *nom de guerre* of Georgi Grigoriev
(1906–1996), *Liberation Nationale et Liberation Sociale:
l'Example de la Revolution Macedonienne,* Collection Anarchiste, Federation Anarchiste, Paris, France, undated.

46 On the anarchists in the Russian Revolt, read Paul Avrich, *The
Russian Anarchists*, Princeton University Press, USA, 1967.

47 For a narrative overview of the history of the ABC, read
Matthew Hart, *Yelenskys' Fable: A History of the ABC,*

Anarchist Black Cross Federation, Los Angeles, USA, 2002.

48 For a brief sketch of the Second and Third Wave IWW, read Michael Hargis, *IWW Chronology 1905–1939*, IWW, USA, originally titled "95 Years of Revolutionary Industrial Unionism," reprinted in *Anarcho-Syndicalist Review* #27, Champaign, Illinois, USA, probably 2000. For more detailed accounts, read Fred W. Thompson and Patrick Murfin, *The IWW: its First 70 Years*, IWW, Chicago, 1976, and Philip S Foner, *The Industrial Workers of the World, 1905–17*, International Publishers, New York, 1965. For a comparative analysis of the IWW's engagement with the national question in the USA and South Africa, read Peter Cole and Lucien van der Walt, "Crossing the Color Lines, Crossing the Continents: Comparing the Racial Politics of the IWW in South Africa and the United States, 1905–1925," *Safundi: The Journal of South African and American Studies*, Vol. 12, No. 1, New Haven, USA, January 2011.

49 On Japan, the key text is John Crump, *The Anarchist Movement in Japan*, Anarchist-Communist Federation, London, UK, 1996, while detail is added by Matthew Turner, *Museifushugi: a Brief History of Anarchism in pre-War Japan*, Libertarian Press, New Zealand, undated.

50 On China, the key text is Arif Dirlik, *Anarchism in the Chinese Revolution*, University of California Press, Berkley, USA, 1991, who explores the national question in "Anarchism and the Question of Place: Thoughts from the Chinese experience," in Hirsch and van der Walt, 2010. On the cultural roots and disputes of the early Chinese anarchist movement read Dirlik's chapter in Gutiérrez Dantón (ed), due in 2013. Other texts include Robert Scalpino & George T. Yu, *The Chinese Anarchist Movement*, Insurgency Culture Collective, Los Angeles, USA, 1999, first published 1961, and Peter Zarrow, *Anarchism and Chinese Political Culture*, Columbia University Press, New York, USA, 1990.

51   On Korea, read Dongyoun Hwang, "Korean Anarchism before 1945: A regional and transnational approach," in Hirsch and van der Walt, 2010, while on the influence of the national liberation struggle on Korea, read the Dongyoun Hwang chapter in Gutiérrez Dantón (ed), due in 2013.

52   The most detailed account of the key debates of the Amsterdam Congress is to be found in Nestor McNab (ed), *The International Anarchist Congress, Amsterdam, 1907*, online at www.fdca.it/fdcaen/press/pamphlets/sla-5/sla-5. pdf, a translated selection of extracts from Maurizio Antonioli, *Dibattito sul Sindicalismo: Atti del Congresso Internazionale Anarchico di Amsterdam (1907)*, Italy, 1978.

53   The current organisation of the FA is online at www.federation-anarchiste.org, the CGA is online at www.c-g-a. org the OCL is online at oclibertaire.free.fr and AL is online at www.alternativelibertaire.org.

54   On the Second, Third, and Fourth Wave FORA in all its permutations, read Antonio López, *La F.O.R.A. en el Movimiento Obrero*, Tupac Ediciones, Buenos Aires, Argentina, 1998, which covers 1903 to about 1968; and Ronaldo Munck, Ricardo Falcon and Bernardo Galitelli, *Argentina: from Anarchism to Perónism—Workers, Unions and Politics 1855–1985*, Zed Books, London, UK, 1987. A study of dockyard syndicalism is Geoffroy de Laforcade, "Straddling the Nation and the Working World: anarchism and syndicalism on the docks and rivers of Argentina," in Hirsch and van der Walt, 2010. The classic work is Diego Abad de Santillán, *La FORA: Ideologíca y Trayectoria del Movimiento Obrero Revolucionario en la Argentina*, Libros de Anarres, Buenos Aires, Argentina, 2007, first published 1933, which covers 1903–1930. A brief overview is provided by Peter Yerril and Leo Rosser, *Revolutionary Unionism: the FORA in Argentina*, ASP, London, UK, 1987.

55   On the Second Wave / early Third Wave FORU, read Astrid Wessels, "From Theatre Groups to Bank

Robberies: the Diverse Experience of Uruguayan Anarchists," Institute for Anarchist Studies, Canada, 2004, online at: www.anarchist-studies.org/articleview/82/1/9.

56 On the Second Wave FORB/COB, read Eric Arthur Gordon, *Anarchism in Brazil: Theory and Practice 1890–1920*, doctoral dissertation, Tulane University, USA, 1978. Brazil is an enormous country and its anarchist movement was and remains very geographically dispersed and ethnically diverse, so for the study of one anarchist citadel alone, read Edilene Toledo and Luigi Biondi, "Constructing Syndicalism and Anarchism Globally: the transnational making of the syndicalist movement in São Paulo, Brazil, 1895–1935," in Hirsch and van der Walt, 2010, and J. Wolfe, *Working Women, Working Men: São Paulo and the rise of Brazil's Industrial Working Class, 1900–1955,* Duke University Press, Durham, USA, 1993. A brief country overview is given by Edgar Rodrigues, Renato Ramos, and Alexandre Samis, *Against all Tyranny! Essays on Anarchism in Brazil,* translated by Paul Sharkey, Kate Sharpley Library, London, UK, 2003.

57 On the utopian, popular liberal, and socialist roots of the Chilean anarchist movement, read the Sergio Grez chapter in Gutiérrez Dantón (ed), due in 2013, while on the Second Wave FTCh/FORCh, read José Antonio Gutiérrez Dantón, "Anarchism in Chile 1872–1995," a synopsis of Hector Pavelic's 1994 book *Caliche: el Rostro Pampino (Saltpetre: the Pampas' Face)*, published in *Black Flag,* London, UK, 1995, online at: www.libcom.org/articles/anarchism-in-chile/index.php while Oscar Ortiz, *Cronica Anarquista de la Subversión Olvidada,* Ediciones Espíritu Libertario, Chile, 2002, covers the Second to Fourth Waves: the 1900s to the 1960s.

58 On the Second Wave FORPa/CORP, read the work of Paraguay's premier anarcho-syndicalist, the typographer Ciriaco Duarte (1908–1996), *Hombres y Obras del Sindicalismo Libre en Paraguay,* Asunción, Paraguay, 1965; and

Rafael Peroni (ed), Ciriaco Duarte, *El Sindicalismo Libre en Paraguay*, Asunción, Paraguay, 1987.

59   On the Second Wave FOH/CTC, read Fernández, 2001; and on their Second Wave forerunners and their inter-connectivity with US anarchists and the IWW, read Carlos D. Pérez de Alejo, "Beyond the Island: a Transnational History of Cuban Anarchism, 1880–1914," MA thesis, University of Texas, Austin, USA, 2008.

60   On the roots of the Mexican movement, as a factor of indigenous resistance in a peripheral country to global capital, read the Brenda Aguilar chapter in Gutiérrez Dantón (ed), due in 2013; while on the Second Wave / early Third Wave COM/FORM/CGT, read Hart, 1978.

61   On the emergence of the Peruvian movement from within the radical liberal tradition and its adaptation to peasant struggles, read the Franz García chapter in Gutiérrez Dantón (ed), due in 2013; while on the Second Wave FORPe/FOL, read Steven J. Hirsch, "Peruvian Anarcho-Syndicalism: Adapting Transnational Influences and Forging Counterhegemonic Practices, 1905–1930," in Hirsch and Van der Walt, 2010.

62   On the emergence of Colombian anarcho-syndicalism from radical nationalism, read the Diego Paredes chapter on Colombia in Gutiérrez Dantón (ed), due in 2013. On the Second Wave FOC, read Luis Alfredo Burbano, Mauricio Flórez Pinzón and Diego Paredes Goicochea, *Presente y pasado del anarquismo y del anarcosindicalismo en Colombia*, Libro de Anarres, Buenos Aires, Argentina, undated.

63   The roots of the Bolivian movement will be discussed by Silvia Rivera Cusicanqui in *Las Vertiente de la Anarquía*, Libros de Anarres, Buenos Aires, Argentina, (due in 2013). On the rather unique feminist-indigenist anarchism of Bolivia, read Marcia Stephenson, *Gender and Modernity in Andean Bolivia*, University of Texas Press, Texas, USA, 1999, and listen to "Indigenous Anarchism in Bolivia: An interview with Silvia Rivera Cusicanqui,"

Rustbelt Radio, Pittsburgh, USA, 2007, online at: http://
pittsburgh.indymedia.org/news/2007/03/26831.php.

64 On the Second and Third Wave Ecuadoran movement,
read Alexei Páez, *El anarquismo en el Ecuador,* Corpo-
ración Editora Nacional, Quito, Ecuador, 1986.

65 On the Second Wave CNT, the leading new account is
Angel Smith, *Anarchism, Revolution and Reaction: Catalan Labour and the Crisis of the Spanish State, 1898–1923,*
International Studies in Social History, Volume 8, Ber-
ghahn Books, Oxford, UK, 2007.

66 On the Second Wave UON/CGT, the best study is João
Freire, *Freedom Fighters: Anarchist Intellectuals, Work-
ers and Soldiers in Portugal's History,* Black Rose Books,
Montreal, Canada, 2001.

67 His writings can be found in Chaz Bufe and Mitchell
Cowen Verter (eds), *Dreams of Freedom: A Ricardo Flores
Magón Reader,* AK Press, Oakland, USA, 2005. A Span-
ish-language online archive of Magónista materials is at
www.archivomagon.net/. On his influence, read Salvador
Hernández Padilla, *El Magónismo: historia de una passion
libertaria 1900–1922,* Ediciones Era, Mexico City, 1984.

68 On the British movement, read Bob Holton, *British Syndicalism 1900–1914: Myths and Realities,* Pluto Press,
London, UK, 1976. On Ireland, read Emmet O'Con-
nor, *Syndicalism in Ireland 1917–1923,* Cork University
Press, Cork, Ireland, 1988. The leading Irish nationalist
and syndicalist, James Connolly, was executed for his role
in the 1916 anti-colonial Easter Rising.

69 Eric Hobsbawm, *Revolutionaries,* Abacus, London, UK, 1999.

70 On the RPAU, the best anarchist study is Alexandre Skirda,
*Nestor Makhno, Anarchy's Cossack: the Struggle for Free So-
viets in the Ukraine 1917–1921,* AK Press, Oakland, USA,
2004. The classic partisan study is Peter Arshinov, *History
of the Makhnovist Movement 1918–1921,* Freedom Press,
London, UK, 1987, first published 1923. The class nature

of the RPAU is examined in Colin Darch, *The Makh-novschina, 1917–1921, Ideology, Nationalism and Peas-ant Insurgency in Early 20ᵗʰ Century Ukraine,* PhD thesis, University of Bradford, UK, 1994. Tackling the colonial issue is Aleksandr Shubin, "The Makhnovist Movement and the National Question in the Ukraine, 1917–1921," in Hirsch and van der Walt, 2010. The structure of the RPAU is best described in Vyacheslov Azerov, *Kontrazved-ka: The story of the Makhnovist Intelligence Service,* Black Cat Press, Edmonton, Canada, 2008, Makhno's own in-complete memoirs (up until only 1918) are particularly instructive: *The Russian Revolution in Ukraine,* and *Under the Blows of the Counterrevolution,* Black Cat Press, Ed-monton, Canada, 2008, first published 1929. The survival of a sporadic Makhnovist movement in Ukraine into the 1930s is described in Anatoly V. Dubrovik, D.I. Rublyov, and Szarapow (trans.), *After Makhno,* Kate Sharpley Li-brary, London, UK, 2009.

71   As in Ukraine, Noveselov's detachments and those of the anarchist G.F. Rogov were defeated by the Red Army after helping defeat Admiral Aleksandr Kolchak's White forces, both partisan leaders being killed in action. For an account of the anarchist movement in Siberia, read Frank Mintz's "A Siberian 'Maknovschina'," a review of Anatoli Shtirbul's Russian-language study *The Anarchist Movement in Siberia in the First Quarter of the 20ᵗʰ Cen-tury: Anti-statist Revolt and Non-statist Self-organisation of the Workers* (1996), Mintz's English-language review is online at www.katesharpleylibrary.net/dfn3rg.

72   The IWA is today much-declined from its glory days, but still represents sections in Argentina, Brazil, Britain, France, Germany, Italy, Norway, Poland, Portugal, Russia, Serbia, Slovakia, and Spain, with "Friends of the IWA" branches in Australia, Chile, and Colombia, and is online at www.iwa-ait.org. For the best overview of Second Wave international syndicalism, read Wayne Thorpe, *"The Work-ers Themselves": Revolutionary Syndicalism and International*

Labour, 1913–23, Kluwer Academic Publishers, Dordrecht, The Netherlands, 1989. For an IWA version of the International's history, read Vadim Damier and Malcolm Archibald (trans), *Anarcho-syndicalism in the 20th Century*, Black Cat Press, Edmonton, Canada, 2009, online at http://libcom.org/files/Damier-AS-A4.pdf.

73 *The Platform* is available online in multiple languages, alongside numerous antecedent proto-platformist documents and *especifista* texts, at http://anarchistplatform.wordpress.com.

74 Michael Schmidt and Jack Grancharoff, *Bulgarian Anarchism Armed: the Anarcho-Communist Mass Line Part 1*, Zabalaza Books, Johannesburg, South Africa, 2008, translated into Portuguese as *Anarquismo Búlgaro em Armas: a Linha de Massas Anarco-Comunista Parte 1,* Faísca Publicações Libertarias, São Paulo, Brazil, 2009.

75 The best explanation of the often misrepresented Polish movement is Rafał Chwedoruk's "Polish Anarchism and Anarcho-Syndicalism in the 20th Century," in *New Perspectives on Anarchism, Labour and Syndicalism: the Individual, the National and the Transnational,* David Berry & Constance Bantman (eds), 2010.

76 On the roots of the Italian anarchist movement—the influence of which was global—and its debates with republicanism during the *Risorgimento*, read the Gino Caraffi chapter in Gutiérrez Dantón (ed), due in 2013. On the *Bienno Rosso*, read "Anarchists in the Italian Factory Occupations," Ian McKay, *Anarcho-Syndicalist Review* No.46, USA, Spring 2007. *The Anarchist FAQ* at http://en.wikibooks.org/wiki/Anarchist_FAQ/What_is_Anarchism%3F/5.5 has greater detail. The influence of the libertarian Marxist Antonio Gramsci on this period is vastly overinflated in many accounts: in reality, his tiny group's journal *L'Ordine Nuovo (The New Order)* had a fortnightly circulation of only 5,000 in 1920—compared to the anarchist UAI newspaper *Umanita Nova*

(*New Humanity*) which circulated 50,000 copies daily in 1920 (the leading liberal newspaper *Corriere della sera* circulated 450,000 daily).

77   On this crucial period in Germany, read: *Syndicalism and Anarcho-Syndicalism in Germany*, Helge Döhring, FAU, Germany, translated by John Carroll, Anarcho-Syndicalism 101, USA, 2006; and Wayne Thorpe, "Keeping the Faith: the German Syndicalists in the First World War," *Central European History*, Vol.33, No.2, undated.

78   John Crump, *Anarchism and Nationalism in East Asia*, York University Press, York, UK, 1995; Dongyoun Hwang, "Reflections on Radicalism in 'Eastern Asia: Regional Perspective, Transnational Approach, and 'Eastern Asia' as a Regional Concept," *The Journal of Korean Studies*, Vol. 145, March 2009, (in Korean).

79   Strangely, there is no adequate overview of the anarchist/syndicalist movement in Latin America, its primary stronghold. The best sources are: Carlos M. Rama and Angel J. Cappelletti, *El Anarquismo en America Latina*, Biblioteca Ayachucho, Caracas, Venezuela, 1990 (Spanish language); S. Fanny Simon, "Anarchism and Anarcho-syndicalism in South America," *The Hispanic American Historical Review*, New York City, USA, 1946; Ian R. Mitchell, "The Anarchist Tradition in Latin America," *Anarchy*, No.79, Express Printers, London, UK, 1979. Luis Vitale, *Contribución a una historia del anarquismo en America Latina*, Editiones, Instituto de Investigación de Movimientos Sociales "Pedro Vuskovic," Santiago, Chile, 1998, is available online at http://mazinger.sisib.uchile.cl/repositorio/lb/filosofia_y_humanidades/vitale/obras/sys/aaml/t.pdf—but has a strong focus on Chile.

80   The only overarching insider account available in English is Ha Ki-Rak, *History of [the] Korean Anarchist Movement*, Anarchist Publishing Committee, Korean Anarchist Federation, Taegu, Korea, 1986, but it suffers from poor structure and analysis; a more coherent account should

be Michael Schmidt, *Korean Anarchism Armed: The An-archo-communist Mass Line Part 3* (forthcoming).

81 The standard CNT history is José Peirats, *The Anarchists in the Spanish Revolution*, Freedom Press, London, 1990, first published in three volumes as *La CNT en la revolu-ción española,* 1951–1953.

82 The most detailed and devastating anarchist critique of the CNT-FAI's failure is Stuart Christie, *We! The Anarchists: A Study of the Iberian Anarchist Federation (FAI)1927–1937,* The Meltzer Press & Jura Media, Hastings, UK & Petersham North, Australia, 2000.

83 Today it is known today simply as the Anarchist Federation (AF) and is online at www.afed.org.uk.

84 A summary of the JAF's history can be found at libcom. org/library/wot-organization; on the FFLU and CLU. read Marshall, 2008.

85 Documentary film by Daniel Goude and Guillaume Lenormant, *Une résistance oubliée (1954–1957), des lib-ertaires dans la guerre d'Algérie,* Alternative Libertaire, Paris, France, 2001, available for purchase online at boutique.alternativelibertaire.org/produit.php?ref=D-VD_Algerie&id_rubrique=5; Schmidt and Van der Walt, 2011.

86 José Peirats, *Appendix* to his *The Anarchists in the Span-ish Revolution,* Black & Red, Detroit, Michigan, 1993; Peirats, "Spanish Anarchism in Exile," in *The Raven Anar-chist Quarterly No.23*, Freedom Press, London, UK, 1993.

87 Ha, 1986.

88 Archives of the *Centre International de Recherches sur l'An-archisme* (CIRA), Lausanne, Switzerland.

89 Sam Dolgoff, *The Cuban Revolution: a Critical Perspec-tive,* Black Rose Books, Montreal, Canada, 1996, on-line at http://dwardmac.pitzer.edu/anarchist_archives/bright/dolgoff/cubanrevolution/toc.html.

90 On Castro's youthful enthusiasm for Benito Mussolini and his adult fascination for and friendship with Juan Perón, for whom he declared three days of national mourning on his death, read *The Boys from Dolores: Fidel Castro and His Generation—From Revolution to Exile*, Patrick Symmes, Robinson, London, UK, 2007. For an account of Castro's friendship with Manuel Fraga Iribarne, read *Ghosts of Spain: Travels Through a Country's Hidden Past*, Giles Tremlett, Faber & Faber, London, UK, 2006.

91 A potted history of the Swedish syndicalist movement can be found in English here: Ingemar Sjöö, *SAC and Syndicalism*, Stockholm-Gotland SAC, Sweden, undated, online at www.sac.se.

92 Interview in 2010 by Michael Schmidt with Chilean anarchist historian and activist José Antonio Gutierrez Dantón, author of *Anarchism in Chile 1872–1995*, a synopsis of Hector Pavelic's 1994 book *Caliche: el Rostro Pampino, (Saltpetre: the Pampas' Face)*, published in *Black Flag*, London, UK, 1995, online at: www.libcom.org/articles/anarchism-in-chile/index.php.

93 On Argentina, read Abad de Santillán, 2005. On New Zealand, read Dick Scott, *151 Days: The Great Waterfront Lockout and Supporting Strikes, February 15–July 15, 1951*, Reed Books, Auckland, New Zealand, 2001.

94 Interview with Chinese anarchist H.L. Wei, a comrade of Chu Cha-Pei's, in Paul Avrich, *Anarchist Voices: an Oral History of Anarchism in America*, AK Press, Oakland, USA, 2005.

95 Ineke Dibits, Elizabeth Paredo, Ruth Volgger, and Ana Cecilia Wadsworth, *Polleras Libertarias: Federación Obrera Femenina, 1927–1964*, Taller de Historia y Participación de la Mujer, La Paz, Bolivia, 1986.

96 Lucien van der Walt, "The First Globalisation and Transnational Labour Activism in Southern Africa: White Labourism, the IWW and the ICU, 1904–1934," *African*

Studies, Johannesburg, South Africa, 2007, online at http://abahlali.org/files/ICU.pdf.

97 Michael Schmidt, "Uruguayan Anarchism Armed: the Anarcho-communist Mass Line Part 2" (forthcoming); the primary insider account is by FAU/OPR-33 veteran Juan Carlos Mechoso, *Acción Directa Anarquista: Una Historia de FAU Tomo II La Fundación,* 2005; *Acción Directa Anarquista: Una Historia de FAU Tomo III Los Primeros Años,* 2006; *Acción Directa Anarquista: Una Historia de FAU,* undated but probably 2002; all Recortes Editorial, Montevideo, Uruguay; I interviewed Mechoso in Porto Alegre, Brazil, in 2003.

98 Ha, 1984.

99 The best introduction to Guillén is Donald C. Hodges (ed & trans), *Philosophy of the Urban Guerrilla: The Revolutionary Writings of Abraham Guillén,* William Morrow, New York, USA, 1973, originally published as *Estragegias de la guerrilla urbana,* Manuales del Pueblo, Montevideo, Uruguay, 1966.

100 On the MIR of Chile, read Ferrada-Noli, *Notas Sobre la Historia del MIR,* online in Spanish with an English summary at http://ferradanoli.files.wordpress.com/2010/08/marcello-ferrada-noli-nelson-gutierrez-historia-del-mir.pdf. See also Ortiz, 2002, who draws on Luis Vitale, *Contribución a la Historia del MIR (1965–1970),* Ediciones Instituto de Investigaciones de Movimientes Sociales, Chile, 1999. An interview with the CUAC is online at www.fdca.it/fdcaen/international/cuac.htm. On the fate of the FAU and OPR-33 of Uruguay, read Juan Carlos Mechoso, Jaime Prieto, Hugo Cores, and others, *The Federación Anarquista Uruguaya (FAU): Crisis, Armed Struggle and Dictatorship, 1967–1985,* Paul Sharkey (ed & trans), Kate Sharpley Library, London, UK, 2009; J. Patrice McSherry, "Death Squads as Parallel Forces: Uruguay, Operation Condor, and the United States," *Journal of Third World Studies,* USA, 2007. On Libertarian

Resistance of Argentina, read Verónica Diz and Fernando López Trujillo, *Resistencia Libertaria*, Editorial Madreselva, Buenos Aires, Argentina, 2007; their account is challenged, however, by RL veterans such as Maria Ester Tello. Also, RL veteran Fernando López interviewed by Chuck Morse, "Resistencia Libertaria: Anarchist Opposition to the Last Argentine Dictatorship," *New Formulation*, USA, 2003, online at www.newformulation. org/3morselopez.htm.

101 In 2004, in Johannesburg, South Africa, I interviewed SB, a *Shagila* veteran who fought in the Iranian Revolution, who also spoke about the Iranian CHK. The true importance of the Iraqi and Iranian anarchist movements, both of which came into being totally without outside influence, has yet to be properly estimated.

102 On the Angry Brigade in the UK, read Jean Weir, *The Angry Brigade, 1967–1984: Documents and Chronology*, Elephant Editions, London, UK, 1978. On Direct Action of France, the best memoir is Jean-Marc Rouillan, *De Memoria (I) Los comienzos: otoño de 1970 en Toulouse* and *De Memoria (II) El duelo de la innocencia: un día de septiembre de 1973 en Barcelona*, Virus Editorial, Barcelona, Spain, undated; while the best analysis is Michael York Dartnell, *Mirror of Violence: The Revolutionary Terrorism of Action Directe as an Element in the Evolution of French Political Culture, 1979–1987*, PhD thesis, York University, North York, Canada, 1993. On Direct Action of Canada, the insider account is Ann Hansen, *Direct Action: Memoirs of an Urban Guerrilla*, AK Press, Oakland, USA, 2002; plus Eryk Martin, *Burn It Down!: A History of Anarchism, Activism, and the Politics of "Direct Action," 1972–1988*, dissertation (forthcoming). On the German M2J, the insider account is Ralf Reinders and Ronald Fritsch, *El Movimiento 2 de Junio: Conversaciones sobre los Rebeldes del Hachís, el secuestro de Lorenz y la cárcel*, Virus Editorial, Barcelona, Spain, undated; plus Inge Viett, *Nie war ich furchtloser: Autobiographie*, Editions Nautilus,

Hamburg, Germany, 1997. On the Basque KAA, read Buzz Burrell, *Insurrection in Euskadi: Political Struggles in the Basque Country*, Partisan Press, Glasgow, UK, 1993.

103 On the pan-European resistance to Franco, the best English sources include: Antonio Téllez and Stuart Christie, *Anarchist International Action Against Francoism From Genoa 1949 to The First Of May Group*, Kate Sharpley Library, UK, 2010; also Octavio Alberola, Alvaro Milán, and Juan Zambrana, *Revolutionary Activism: The Spanish Resistance in Context*, Kate Sharpley Library, UK, 2000; and André Cortade, *1000: histoire désordonnée du M.I.L., Barcelone 1967–1974*, Dérive 17, Paris, 1985; in 2011, I interviewed sole surviving DI Council member Octavio Alberola Suriñach, Perpignan, France, for the book *The People Armed: Anarchist Guerrillas Verbatim*, AK Press, Oakland, USA (forthcoming).

104 The MLCE, its name today shortened to MLC, was founded in 1961, and today has a presence in Mexico, Venezuela, France and Spain, with underground contacts in Cuba itself. Not to be confused with a *lasses-faire* capitalist organisation of the same name founded by Cuban exile businessmen in Miami, USA, in 1981, its website is at www.mlc.acultura.org.ve.

105 On anarchism during the "Dirty War" period in Mexico in the 1960s and 1970s and how it shaped indigenous struggles for autonomy in Chiapas and Oaxaca today, read the Brenda Aguilar chapter in Gutiérrez Dantón (ed), due in 2013.

106 Phillip Ruff, *Anarchy in the USSR: A New Beginning*, ASP, London, UK, 1991; Mikhail Tsovma, "Remembering Natalia Pirumova," Centre International de Recherches sur l'Anarchisme, *Bulletin 63*, Lausanne, Switzerland, September 2007.

107 The Polish FA is still operational, and is online at www.federacja-anarchistyczna.pl. The CSAF is online at www.csaf.cz. In 1997, the Federation of Social Anarchists

(FSA) split from the CSAF and affiliated to the IWA and now appears to be defunct. The ASF split in 1996, into the platformist Organisation of Revolutionary Anarchists—Solidarity (ORA-S) and the purist Czechoslovak Federation of Revolutionary Anarchists (SFRA); in 2003, a platformist minority in ORA-S broke away and founded Anarcho-Communist Alternative (AKA), aka. anarchokomunismus.org while the remainder of ORA-S turned towards ultra-leftist Marxism. On FOSATU, read Sian Byrne, "'Building Tomorrow Today': a re-examination of the character of the controversial 'workerist' tendency associated with the Federation of South African Trade Unions (FOSATU) in South Africa, 1979–1985," MA research report, University of the Witwatesrrand, Johannesburg, (in process).

108 Autonomous Action's English website is online at: avtonom.org/en

109 For my analysis of the tactics and strategies of *especifismo* in Latin America, read Michael Schmidt, "Fire-ants and Flowers: Revolutionary Anarchism in Latin America," ZACF, Johannesburg, South Africa, 2004, online at nefac.net/node/38. The most detailed exposition of *especifismo*, however, is "Social Anarchism and Organisation," Anarchist Federation of Rio de Janeiro (FARJ), 2008, online in English at www.anarkismo.net/article/22150.

110 The founding statement of PALIR of Senegal was given to me courtesy of Mitch Miller of the Workers' Solidarity Alliance, USA. According to a 1981 report in the Vancouver, Canada, libertarian socialist journal *The Open Road*, the Senegalese anarchists originally published their manifesto in the Senegalese journal *Le Politicien*. A few brief reports on the IWW Sierra Leone are available at flag.blackened.net/revolt/africa/sierra/sl_iww_update. html. My obituary of Choongo is online at: libcom.org/ history/choongo-wilstar-1964-1999. On the Awareness League of Nigeria, read Sam Mbah (b. 1963) & I.E. Igariwey, *African Anarchism: The History of a Movement*,

See Sharp Press, Tucson, USA, 1997, online at www.
adnauseam.fr/african-anarchism-the-history-of-a,012.
html?lang=fr. Several documents from the Awareness
League are available online at flag.blackened.net/revolt/
africa/aware.html. Mbah is still active and has a blog at
sammbah.wordpress.com/. On the revived Southern African movement, read the NEFAC interview with myself,
online at zabnew.wordpress.com/2010/12/02/nefac-in-
terviews-the-bmc. The ZACF of South Africa is online at
www.zabalaza.net.

111 Common Struggle (USA) is online at www.nefac.net,
Common Cause (Ontario) is online at linchpin.ca and
UCL (Québec) is online at www.causecommune.net.

112 The CGT of Spain is online at www.cgt.es. The SKT
of Siberia is online at syndikalist.narod.ru. The CNT-
France is online at www.cnt-f.org. The SAC of Sweden
is online at www.sac.se. The Italian Confederation of the
Base—United Committees of the Base (CIB-UNICO-
BAS) Italy is online at www.cib-unicobas.it. The French
SUD Education Union's website is at www.sudeducation.
org. FESAL-E's Italian website is at www.fesal.it, but does
not seem to have been active since 2009.

113 The old ILS webpage on its projects in Latin America is
mirrored at www.fdca.it/fdcaen/ILS/ils_projects.htm.

114 The multilingual anarkismo project is online at www.
anarkismo.net.

115 On the Alternative Libertaire section in French Guyana,
read "Interview with Alternative Libertaire in French
Guyana," online at www.nefac.net/node/1734. The
Eastern Mediterranean Libertarian Collective (EMLC)
of Israel/Palestine is online at www.shalif.com/anar-
chy. The Libertarian Communist Alternative (*al-Badil
al-Chouyouii al-Taharoui*) of Lebanon can be found online at albadilaltaharrouri.wordpress.com; also read Michael Schmidt, "Eyewitness Lebanon: In the Land of the
Blind: Hezbollah Worship, Slavish Anti-imperialism and

the Need for a Real Alternative," 2006, online at www.
anarkismo.net/newswire.php?story_id=3651. On Iran,
read "Interview with an Iranian Anarchist," interview
with "Payman Piedar," editor of the No God/State/Master (*Nakhdar*) Iranian exile network in the USA 2005,
online at www.anarkismo.net/article/584. The Swaziland
section of the ZACF was shut down in 2007, but the
Zimbabwean *Uhuru* Network's blog is online at www.
toyitoyi.blogspot.com. "Egypt: Birth of the Libertarian
Socialist Movement, Egypt," 2011, with an analysis of
this minimum-position manifesto by Michael Schmidt,
online at www.anarkismo.net/article/19666.

116 *Manifest pour une Alternative Libertaire* is online at www.
alternativelibertaire.org/spip.php?rubrique23.

117 The English version of Saverio Crapraro's *Anarchist-Communists: A Question of Class*, FdCA, Italy, 2005, is online
at www.fdca.it/fdcaen/organization/theory/acqoc/index.
htm. The ZACF of South Africa later produced a critique, "Tangled Threads of Revolution: Reflections on
A Question of Class," James Pendlebury, South Africa,
online at theanarchistlibrary.org/HTML/James_Pendlebury__Tangled_Threads_of_Revolution.html.

118 Rosa Luxemburg (1871–1919) was a Polish anti-Bolshevik "left communist" economist. "Organisational Questions of the Russian Social Democracy" is online at www.
marxists.org/archive/luxemburg/1904/questions-rsd/
index.htm.

ABOUT THE AUTHOR

Michael Schmidt (born in Johannesburg, 1966) is an anarchist-communist journalist, grassroots organiser, ideologue, historian, and international activist. Raised by a middle-class white family, Schmidt was drafted into the apartheid South African Defence Force in 1985 at the time of the Insurrection. It was this experience that radicalised him, leading him to become a conscientious objector and face a military tribunal chaired by a Supreme Court judge in Pretoria for refusing to serve in 1991. That experience drove his ideology leftwards and he embraced anarchism.

Today, Schmidt is the Executive Director of the Institute for the Advancement of Journalism and Administrative Secretary of the Professional Journalists' Association of South Africa. An active participant in the international anarchist milieu, he is the co-author, with Lucien van der Walt, of *Black Flame: The Revolutionary Class Politics of Anarchism and Syndicalism*, published in 2009 by AK Press. A companion volume, *Global Fire: 150 Fighting Years of Anarchism and Syndicalism*, will be published by AK Press in 2015.

He lives and works in Johannesburg, South Africa.